MICHELLE LAW is a writer and actor working in print, screen and stage. Her plays include the highly acclaimed *Single Asian Female* (La Boite), which toured widely and has had multiple productions, and *Top Coat* (Sydney Theatre Company). Michelle co-created, co-wrote and starred in the award-winning web series *Homecoming Queens* for SBS On Demand (AWG Best Web Series; Melbourne Web Fest Best Screenplay; Equity Ensemble Awards Best Performance in a Comedy Series; AACTA Awards Best Online Video or Series nomination). As a screenwriter, Michelle has worked on shows for ABC, SBS, Fox, Network 10, The Nine Network, and Netflix. Some of her television credits include *Safe Home* (SBS), *The Bureau of Magical Things* (Network 10), *Rosehaven* (ABC), and *Get Krack!n* (ABC). Her awards include two Australian Writers Guild Awards, the Queensland Premier's Young Publishers and Writers Award, and the Arts & Culture 40 Under 40 Awards, which celebrates the country's most influential Asian Australians. Michelle is also a widely published freelance author and a prolific speaker on panels and at festivals. Her first book, *Asian Girls are Going Places*, was published by Hardie Grant in 2022.

L–R: Michelle Law, Jing-Xuan Chan, Mabel Li and Shirong Wu in Belvoir's production of MISS PEONY. (Photo: Brett Boardman)

Miss Peony

Michelle Law

CURRENCY PRESS
The performing arts publisher

BELVOIR ST THEATRE

CURRENT THEATRE SERIES

First published in 2023
by Currency Press Pty Ltd,
PO Box 2287, Strawberry Hills, NSW, 2012, Australia
enquiries@currency.com.au
www.currency.com.au

in association with Belvoir Theatre.

Typeset by Brighton Gray for Currency Press.
Cover image shows Shirong Wu, Michelle Law, Gabrielle Chan;
photo by Daniel Boud; cover design by Alphabet Studio.

Currency Press acknowledges the Traditional Owners of the Country on which
we live and work. We pay our respects to all Aboriginal and Torres Strait
Islander Elders, past and present.

A catalogue record for this
book is available from the
National Library of Australia

NATIONAL
LIBRARY
OF AUSTRALIA

Contents

L–R: Kristina Chan, Courtney Stewart and Nicole Pingon in Belvoir's production of MISS PEONY. (Photo: Brett Boardman)

Charles Wu and Michelle Law in Belvoir's production of MISS PEONY. (Photo: Brett Boardman)

Writer's Note

Miss Peony was written over the course of several years, but the concept for it was seeded more than two decades ago.

I was eleven years old and visiting family in Hong Kong. My Kow Foo, Kum Moh, Biu Goh and I were watching the Miss Hong Kong pageant on TV, my jaw on the floor the entire time. Because I was born in and had grown up in Australia, I'd never seen so many Asian women on screen before. It was incredible witnessing so many women who looked like me being celebrated for their appearance and connection to culture when I'd learnt to dislike these things about myself and assimilate in order to survive living in a western country.

One contestant stood out to me: a woman struggling to answer interview questions in Cantonese before ultimately giving up and speaking in English. She had an Australian accent. I remember sitting straighter on the couch as I watched her. She sounded like an ABC (Australian-Born Chinese) and a banana, just like me—yellow on the outside; white on the inside. She gave me hope that perhaps there was finally a place in the world where I could belong. And then she was eliminated from the pageant.

Miss Peony is a story about the unique sense of displacement experienced by diasporic peoples. It's about the trauma of experiencing exclusion from all sides, and the ways in which we cope with the unspoken judgement and elitism from our own peoples when racial divides demand very narrowed definitions of cultural authenticity. It's also an exploration of intercultural racism and lateral violence among Chinese nationalities. We may be the world's largest ethnic group, but we are not a monolith. The same can be said for our languages.

Translating and surtitling this show has been one of the most exciting, political and challenging experiences of my creative practice to date. I could not be more grateful for our astounding translators Professor Jing Han, Sylvia Xu and Samantha Kwan, who have spent countless hours massaging and troubleshooting this gargantuan task. I hope this script provides encouragement for more productions to attempt to decentralise English and the spoken word while making theatre more inclusive and accessible to historically excluded audiences.

A big thank you to the entire team at Belvoir for embracing *Miss Peony* and new Australian work; to our joyous and generous cast and crew; to Tracey Yu and Reiko Bui for their insights into the pageant universe; to the Asian Australian artists who took part in development workshops for *Miss Peony*; to Louise Gough, Polly Rowe and Carissa Licciardello for their dramaturgically brilliant brains; and finally to director Courtney Stewart. Court, thank you for being there from the very beginning of everything, for being an enduring role model, and for continuing to be the most wonderful friend and collaborator. Thank '*your*', sis.

Michelle Law

Miss Peony was first presented by Belvoir St Theatre, Asia TOPA in association with Arts Centre Melbourne and Queensland Performing Arts Centre at Belvoir, Gadigal country, Sydney, on 1 July 2023, with the following cast:

ADELINE	Gabrielle Chan
MARCY	Jing-Xuan Chan
LILY	Michelle Law
SABRINA	Mabel Li
VINCENT	Charles Wu
JOY	Shirong Wu

Director, Courtney Stewart
Set and Costume Designer, Jonathan Hindmarsh
Lighting Designer, Trent Suidgeest
Composer, Dr Nicholas Ng
Sound Designer, Julian Starr
Choreographer, Kristina Chan
Singing Teacher, Sheena Crouch
Assistant Director, Nicole Pingon
Subtitling & Mandarin Translator, Dr Jing Han
Cantonese Translator, Sylvia Xu

L–R: Jing-Xuan Chan, Mabel Li, Michelle Law and Shirong Wu in Belvoir's production of MISS PEONY. *(Photo: Brett Boardman)*

Jing-Xuan Chan, Shirong Wu, Michelle Law, Charles Wu and Mabel Li in Belvoir's production of MISS PEONY. *(Photo: Brett Boardman)*

CHARACTERS

LILY, 26 years old. An assimilated, Australian-born Chinese woman who rejects the traditional Chinese values with which she was raised. Spiritually lost and searching for acceptance.

ADELINE, deceased. Lily's Por Por (maternal grandmother) who appears as a ghost. Once a Hong Kong beauty queen, and then a prominent member of the Sydney Chinese community.

MARCY, 25 years old. A first-generation migrant from mainland China and a contestant in Miss Peony. Passionate about her family business and single-minded in her pursuit of success.

JOY, 23 years old. A Taiwanese international student and a contestant in Miss Peony. Fiercely intellectual and a loveable oddball. Romantic, and seeking connection in a foreign land.

SABRINA, 18 years old. An Australian-born Chinese LG (Little Girl) from Western Sydney and a contestant in Miss Peony. Grew up idolising Miss Peony winners and is pageant obsessed.

ZHEN HUA, 28 years old. An Australian-born Chinese man who hosts and produces Miss Peony. Cares deeply about his community and works hard to protect it.

NOTE ON LANGUAGE

This script is performed in English, Cantonese, and Mandarin. In production, surtitles are required for these three languages and are played concurrently.

This play text went to press before the end of rehearsals and may differ from the play as performed.

L–R: Jing-Xuan Chan, Mabel Li and Shirong Wu in Belvoir's production of MISS PEONY. (Photo: Brett Boardman)

ACT ONE

SCENE 1

A hospice room.

LILY *finishes a cigarette in the entryway, looking shaken. She waves the smoke away and peers into the room, watching a hospice* NURSE *attend to* ADELINE, *who lies unconscious in bed.* ADELINE *breathes in a way that is slow and laboured; she is close to death.*

LILY: Is she in a lot of pain?

NURSE: She has existential distress. It's very common among palliative-care patients.

LILY: What is that? Existential distress?

NURSE: It could mean a lot of things. She might be struggling with something internally. So it's good she has family with her.

LILY: Right. Can she hear me?

NURSE: [*nodding*] She's even been talking in her more lucid moments. It happens sometimes at the hospice.

LILY: With the stubborn ones, I'm guessing.

NURSE: I was going to say the fighters. How about I give you some time with her?

LILY: Oh you don't need to (go) —!

> *The* NURSE *leaves. Feeling lost,* LILY *paces around the room. Eventually she just goes on her phone.* ADELINE *stirs.*

ADELINE: [*in Cantonese*] 阿囡？ (Daughter?)

LILY: Por Por? It's Lily.

ADELINE: [*in Cantonese*] 冬冬？ (Dong Dong?)

LILY: Mum's gone home to shower. What do you need?

ADELINE: [*in Cantonese*] 快啲、快啲。 (Faster, faster.)

LILY: You're not allowed anymore morphine. Do you want some water?

ADELINE: [*in Cantonese*] 屋企。我想番屋企。 (Home. I want to go home.)

LILY: You can't go home. You have to stay here. How about …

LILY looks around the room, searching for something, anything. She picks up a jade bracelet.

How about your jade bracelet? That's something from home.

She tries sliding the bracelet onto ADELINE*'s wrist but some unknown force repels her. She tries again—same outcome. She puts the bracelet down, unsettled.*

Can you hold on until Mum gets here? I'm sorry it's me here and not her. I should be packing. Most of my things have already been shipped to London. Couch. Clothes. Dining table. My whole life packed into a wooden crate. You don't understand a word I'm saying, do you?

ADELINE: [*in Cantonese*] 冬冬。 (Dong Dong.)

LILY: Yes? Por Por?

ADELINE: [*in Cantonese*] 我聞到陣煙味。唔好食煙。 (I smell smoke. Don't smoke.)

LILY: I wasn't smoking.

ADELINE: [*in Cantonese*] 唔準講大話。你由細到大都咁難湊。從來都唔聽教。不如你應承我一樣嘢。 (Don't lie. You've always been so difficult. Never did as you were told. So promise me something.)

LILY: I can't understand Canto when you're speaking so fast.

ADELINE: [*in Cantonese*] 你一定要攞牡丹小姐嘅冠軍。成為我嘅接班人！呢樣係我唯一想要嘅。傻豬，應承我喇。 (You have to win Miss Peony. Honour my legacy! That's all I've ever wanted. Promise me, silly pig.)

LILY: [*in Cantonese*] 傻豬？ (Silly pig?) You haven't called me that since I was little. I think you're talking about Miss Peony, but why does it matter right now? It's just a stupid community event. Plus, pageants are tacky enough as it is let alone making it a Chinese pageant. At least in England they've got a real sense of class and refinement that they're not faking.

ADELINE: [*distressed, in Cantonese*] 應承我啊，冬冬！ (Promise me, Dong Dong!)

LILY: I promise you! Please just rest.

ADELINE: [*smiling, in Cantonese*] 我嘅傻豬。 (My silly pig.)

ADELINE places the bracelet in LILY*'s hand, wraps* LILY*'s fingers around it.* LILY *holds the bracelet, confused.*

SCENE 2

A casino conference hall.

Adeline's funeral. LILY *arranges programmes and gut yees—envelopes containing candy and a gold coin—on a table with Adeline's photo on it. An elderly* UNCLE *and* AUNTY *approach.* LILY *hands them gut yees and they hand* LILY *an envelope filled with cash.*

LILY: [*in Cantonese*] 有心啦。 (Thank you.) Uncle. Aunty.

UNCLE: Our condolences.

LILY: How are you both? How are you, aunty?

UNCLE: She fine. She going deaf.

AUNTY: Your Por Por live to good age and so proud of you. So happy you compete in Miss Peony.

LILY: I never competed in Miss Peony. You must be thinking of my mum.

AUNTY: Wah, never compete! Such a waste! [*To Uncle, in Cantonese*] 你仲記唔記得阿玲玲姐成日呻佢呀？明明夠醒目可以好似佢阿爸阿媽一樣做醫生，但就偏偏唔肯讀大學。依家做埋管理酒吧呢啲唔正經嘅嘢，又成日淨係同鬼仔拍拖。 (Remember Adeline would always bitch about her? Smart enough to be a doctor like her parents but didn't even go to university. Manages a bar like some low life, and always a revolving door of white boyfriends.)

LILY: So … it's been a long time since we've seen each other.

AUNTY: Yes! So grown up now from the little girl bringing peanuts when we played mah jong. How old are you?

LILY: Twenty-six.

AUNTY: Twenty-six! Then this your last year to enter Miss Peony! Otherwise too old, game over.

She waves a flyer advertising Miss Peony in LILY*'s face.*

AUNTY: Look! Applications open yesterday. You should enter. You not so ugly.

LILY: Miss Peony isn't … my cup of tea.

AUNTY: How you know if you not try the tea!

LILY: I've tried the tea. The tea is cold.

AUNTY: Be good girl. Learn Chinese. Bleach face. Cook more. Marry Chinese boy. Don't you have Chinese friends who can help you?

LILY: No. I don't have many friends, come to think of it. I'm busy at work.

AUNTY: No friends! Wah! The opposite of your Por Por!

UNCLE: [*to Aunty*] All right, leave the girl alone. We're going to miss out on good seats. I want to see who turned up. Probably all of Sydney.

LILY: So nice to see you.

AUNTY: What you have against Miss Peony!

LILY: Bye bye!

AUNTY: [*to Uncle, in Cantonese*] 真係唔敢信嗰個係Lily嚟㗎。有冇見到佢周身都係紋身呀？左青龍右白虎、成個古惑女咁。梗係拍開丸仔。你知啦，傷心傷身。唔怪得知激死阿玲玲姐。 (I can't believe that's Lily. Did you see her tattoos? Visible for everyone to see like a gangster. She's probably on drugs. No doubt she drove Adeline to her death. Heartbreak can kill, you know.)

UNCLE: She had lung cancer from chain-smoking.

AUNTY: [*in Cantonese*] 有個咁嘅孫女呀，係人都會變做老煙鏟！仲要係唯一一粒孫添！佢今年廿六歲啦都仲未嫁得出，冇人冇物，睇嚟都會變籮底橙㗎啦。到時人老珠黃，仲有邊個喉住佢呢隻生唔出蛋嘅雞乸？真係搵鬼呀！佢喺個酒吧蹉跎歲月，諗埋佢梗係嗍懵咗啦。 (Who wouldn't chain-smoke with a granddaughter like that! And her only grandchild! The girl is twenty-six, friendless, unmarried. She's on a one-way track to becoming a leftover woman, and then who will want her and her wrinkly womb? Nobody! She's throwing away her life at that bar. Come to think of it—she has definitely got to be on drugs.)

> *They leave.* LILY *angrily sets up a firepit and burns paper goods: joss paper, paper clothing, a paper house, etc.*

LILY: I'm not on drugs. [*Calling out*] And I can understand some of what you're saying about me! Old bitch. I like my life. I don't need any of you people and I don't need your trashy pageant either. What I need … is a cigarette.

> *She rummages in her bag, searching for a smoke. As she searches, a funeral procession enters. A Chinese* SINGER *performs 'Wind Beneath My Wings', enunciating poorly.*

LILY *finds something unexpected in her bag: Adeline's jade bracelet. She'd forgotten about it. Without thinking, she slips it on. Smoke fills the room ... perhaps from the firepit, perhaps from some otherworldly place.* LILY *doesn't notice. Finally, she finds her cigarettes and exits. With* LILY *gone, smoke continues filling the space and from it emerges a tall and menacing figure. As it edges closer, the lights black out.*

SCENE 3

A hotel room at the casino.

LILY *smokes and channel-surfs on an unseen television. We hear an advertisement for Miss Peony:*

VOICEOVER [*in Cantonese*]「你認為自己有冇資格做下一屆嘅牡丹小姐？你可唔可以成為華人之光，用優雅自豪嘅體態代表我哋社區？即日嚟星河賭場報名競選牡丹小姐啦！」 ('Do you have what it takes to be the next Miss Peony? Will you represent our community with grace and cultural pride? Apply for Miss Peony at Galaxies Casino today!')

LILY *turns the TV off and fixes herself a drink. She sips and stares at the jade bracelet on her arm. When she touches it, there is a loud knock at the door.*

LILY: Hello?

The lights flicker. Sounds of rattling gasps fill the room.

Hello?

The lights flicker off. Sounds of laughter and the howling wind.

Who's there?

LILY *fumbles for the light switch and flicks it on. Before her stands* ADELINE *in a glamorous cheongsam and red lipstick. They clock each other and scream—pure terror and chaos.*

ARGH! OH MY GOD, OH MY GOD, OH MY GOD.

ADELINE: [*in Cantonese*] 乜呢度就係陰間？ 冬冬，你幾時死㗎！ (Is this the afterlife? When did you die, Dong Dong!)

LILY: I'm not dead! YOU'RE the dead one! You—you—you—ZOMBIE!

ADELINE: [*in Cantonese*] 嗦過你把口呀！殭屍啲肉一忽一忽咁跌落嚟咁鬼核突，邊度似係我呀。你望下！我仲係咁貌美如花，梗係變咗隻靚鬼。 (Wash your mouth! Zombies are disgusting, falling apart with flesh wounds everywhere. Look at me! I'm beautiful. I must be a ghost.)

LILY: Ghosts aren't real.

ADELINE: [*in Cantonese*] 嘩！我唔知你畀西方文化點樣洗腦法，但係我哋華人不嬲都知道生同死人係緊密相連㗎。 (Ha! I don't know how Western culture has brainwashed you, but the Chinese have always known that the physical and the spirit world are connected.)

LILY: Por Por—

ADELINE: [*in Cantonese*] 咩呀？做咩事幹？ (What? What is it?)

LILY: We can understand each other's languages. We're having a conversation for the first time. This is incredible.

ADELINE: [*in Cantonese*] 我哋成日傾計㗎喇。 (We've had plenty of conversations.)

LILY: Maybe when I was a kid. Otherwise we never really spoke besides you forcing me to eat.

ADELINE: [*in Cantonese*] 你係咪想我攬下你呀？好似荷里活片入面啲鬼婆咁樣，焗啲藍罐曲奇畀你食呀？你班鬼仔呀，成日喺度情情塔塔，我哋華人掛住搵食，邊有時間嘥喺啲無聊嘢度呀。我親眼見過我啲表兄妹打仗嗰陣生勾勾畀人埋咗。嗰時冇水冇糧，我泥都食過呀，仲要喺啲米田共入面摷種子食。我大把感人嘅故仔畀你嘆呀。 (You wanted me to hug you? Bake some cookies like those white grandmothers in Hollywood movies? You Westerners. So many feelings. Chinese people don't have time for that nonsense. We're too busy surviving. I saw my cousins get buried alive during the war. When there was no food, I ate dirt and seeds scavenged from cowshit. There's some sentimental stories for you.)

LILY: Por Por, what was it like? To die?

ADELINE: [*in Cantonese*] 好得人驚！嗰間病房最後成個監倉咁，啲護士幫我泵枕頭果陣焗住要我聽佢地吹水，話咩一生完仔佢哋啲老公就想要撲嘢。我真係寧願死都唔想再聽到咩嘅男人未割包皮之前，下面成嚿豆皮壽司咁— (Horrible! That hospital room was a prison in the end, hearing the nurses complain about their husbands demanding sex straight after childbirth while they plumped my pillows. Better to die than hear another word about a man's uncircumcised penis looking like a sad snail—)

LILY: What do you want? Why are you here?

ADELINE: [*in Cantonese*] 你話我知先啱呀！肯定我哋之間有件未了嘅事。遊魂野鬼我鍾意去邊都得啦，可以去灣仔食下新鮮出爐嘅蛋撻，又或者可以去濱海灣瘋狂購物。但係依家我就同你喺呢間爛鬼時鐘酒店到，平時啲一樓一實帶啲麻甩佬上嚟咁嘅地方喊啦。我哋上次見係幾時呀？ (You tell me! We must have unfinished business. As a ghost I could be anywhere—eating fresh egg tarts in Wan Chai or shopping at Marina Bay. Instead I'm here with you in this sad hotel room where sex workers bring lonely men to cry. When did we last speak?)

LILY: The day before you died. You'd had a lot of morphine and you were talking about Miss Peony for some reason.

ADELINE: [*in Cantonese*] 我講過啲咩呀？ (What did I say exactly?)

LILY: I couldn't understand most of what you were saying.

ADELINE: [*in Cantonese*] 你睇下，仲唔係你嘅錯？就係因為你唔再講廣東話，將所有精力擺曬去學英文。 (See? Your fault. Because you stopped speaking Cantonese. Put all of your energy into learning English.)

LILY: You made me promise you something.

      ADELINE *gasps.*

ADELINE: [*in Cantonese*] 我記得喇。你應承過我你會攞牡丹小姐嘅冠軍！ (I REMEMBER. You promised me that you would win Miss Peony!)

LILY: What?! That can't be it.

ADELINE: [*in Cantonese*] 哎呀冬冬，真係好喇。有啲人未完成嘅心願係要搞謀殺、復仇啦，好大陣仗。我哋算好彩啦。 (Oh this is good, Dong Dong. Some people's unfinished business is dangerous—like murder and revenge. We got off easy.)

    [*Surveying Lily*] 雖然都有少少難度 ... (Although there will be challenges ...)

LILY: I would never make that promise!

ADELINE: [*in Cantonese*] 咁你話我點解會喺度呀！ (And yet here I am!)

LILY: I'm moving overseas in a week!

ADELINE: [*not listening, in Cantonese*] 唉，我都好掛住選美小姐呢個圈子。我卜卜脆嗰陣呀攞匀晒所有亞洲嘅選美冠軍。喺香港份份雜誌頭版都係我個樣。每個月最少有十個人向我求婚，啲競爭對手妒忌起我上嚟，寄成兩倍嘅恐嚇信俾我呀。曾經有個富豪買咗個私人半島送俾我，另一個仲曾經愛我愛到自殺添。 (Ah, I miss the pageant circuit. In my prime I won every pageant title across Asia. My face was plastered on the cover of every magazine in Hong Kong. Each month, I would receive ten marriage proposals, and twice as many death threats from jealous rivals. One man bought an island for me. Another blew himself up in my name.)

LILY: Por Por, are you hearing me?! I don't have time to enter Miss Peony! I'm moving to London next week!

ADELINE: [*in Cantonese*] 咁我都要執包袱走人呀！你知喇，我成日都想去英國旅行。睇下啲守衛交更啦，同大笨鐘影下相啦。同我個孫女周圍觀光，可以行成世啦。 (I should pack my bags, then! You know, I've always wanted to visit England. Watch the changing of the guards. Pose with Big Ben. See the sights with my granddaughter. For eternity.)

LILY: You can't be serious. Miss Peony is horrible! It's all the fakeness and bluntness and nosiness of the Chinese community on meth! Not to mention I don't agree with pageants on principle! They're shallow, and sexist—

ADELINE: [*in Cantonese*] 牡丹小姐嘅宗旨係成為華人之光！係為咗我哋嘅社區！你明唔明？如果你唔遵守承諾，我哋倆個有排煩啊。之前我有個老友俾佢個死鬼信佛老公纏咗成世，就因為佢臨死之前應承咗以後會改食齋。但係佢就做唔到喇。KFC個Zinger Box實在太好食啦。 (Miss Peony is about cultural pride! Community! Don't you understand? If you don't fulfill your promise, we both suffer. A childhood friend of mine was haunted by her Buddhist husband for the rest of her life because she promised him that she would go vegetarian after he died. She couldn't do it. She loves the KFC Zinger Box.)

LILY *picks up her cigarette.* ADELINE *stubs it out.*

[*In Cantonese*] 唔準食煙呀！你唔記得我係生cancer死咖！ (No smoking! I died from lung cancer!)

LILY: Por Por! I can't do it!

ADELINE: [*in Cantonese*] 你驚咩啊？ (What are you afraid of?)

LILY: Look at me. Even if I entered Miss Peony I wouldn't know where to start.

ADELINE: [*in Cantonese*] 你只要跟足我講嘅做就得啦！我會照我自己嘅形象去塑造你。 (Start by doing everything I say! I will mould you in my image.)

LILY: I don't want to be moulded.

ADELINE: [*in Cantonese*] 咁你就乜機會都冇啦。你知唔知你輸咗會點呀？我成世都會塞喺度做遊魂嘢鬼啊。 (Then you won't stand a chance. Do you know what will happen if you lose? I will be stuck in purgatory forever.)

LILY: So what?

ADELINE: [*in Cantonese*] 咁呀，同你嚮往嘅倫敦新生活講拜拜喇，因為我做鬼都唔會放過你㗎。你去到邊我就跟到邊。呢啲就叫做撞鬼喇。你嘅一舉一動我都會望實。我會批評你每一個決定。如果因為你唔遵守諾言搞到我上唔到天堂，我一定會搞到你冇啖好食，冇覺好瞓。 (So, say goodbye to your shiny new life in London because I will be dragged along there with you. Wherever you go, I must go. Those are the rules of hauntings. Every movement you make I will be watching. Every decision you make I will be criticising. If you fail to keep your promise and I can't get into heaven, then I will make your life a living hell.)

LILY: Didn't you do enough of that when you were alive?!

ADELINE: [*in Cantonese*] 如果你真係咁諗就聽我講！我作為牡丹小姐嘅靈魂人物，係所有佳麗啲偶像。有我幫你實贏啦。 (If that's how you feel, then listen to me! I was the heart and soul of Miss Peony—a champion for contestants to aspire to. With my help, you will win.)

A beat as LILY *considers.*

LILY: If I do everything you say, you'll leave me alone? You won't come to London with me? You'll disappear?

ADELINE: [*in Cantonese*] 係呀。如果你乖乖地聽話，你一定會贏牡丹小姐。到時我就唔會再纏你纏成世。咁你同唔同意我嘅條件呀？ (Yes. If you do everything I say, you will win Miss Peony. I will leave you alone. Forever. So do you agree to my terms or not?)

LILY: [*acquiescing*] Do I have a choice?

SCENE 4

Casino conference hall.

The morning after. Miss Peony applicants are scattered around the room completing entry forms. MARCY *and* JOY *eye each other off and then smile shyly when they catch each other's gaze.* SABRINA *confers with* ZHEN HUA. LILY *enters with* ADELINE *and takes everything in. She tries leaving but* ADELINE *magically spins her back around.*

LILY: There's so many people here! This is too hard.

ADELINE: [*in Cantonese*] 邊度難啊！不知幾刺激！ (It's not hard! It's exciting!)

> ADELINE *begins appraising the other women, invisible to them.*

[*In Cantonese*] 嚆，望實啦，呢啲就係你嘅競爭對手！我識呢個女仔—佢叫梁瑪斯。有錢女嚟，佢又櫻桃小嘴，隻眼仔又圓碌碌咁，實去過韓國加工。你要買啲雙眼皮貼。 (Look, see, here is your competition! I know this girl—Marcy Liang. Comes from a very wealthy background. She has a delicate mouth and nice, big eyes—probably got double eyelid surgery in Korea. You'll need to buy some eyelid tape.)

> *Next is* JOY.

[*In Cantonese*] 呢個女仔有前有後，著旗袍嗰個環節一定會曬身材。啲人成日話亞洲人新陳代謝得快，但係睇下你老豆。你似足佢咁啊，所以由而家開始唔俾再食溦粉質。 (This girl has a nice figure—she'll show it off in the cheongsam round. Everyone talks about Asian metabolisms being fast but look at your father. You take after him so from here onwards, cut out carbohydrates from your diet.)

> *Next is* SABRINA.

[*In Cantonese*] 都話一白遮三醜，呢個女仔幾好呀，啲皮膚滑捋捋咁。你望下你塊面啲雀斑呀！記得以後每日出門口搽防曬呀。同埋快啲戒煙。 (This girl has lovely, clear skin. Nice and white, too. Look at the pigmentation on your cheeks! You need to wear sunscreen every day. And make sure you quit smoking.)

> *Next, she checks out* ZHEN HUA.

[*In Cantonese*] 哇望下呢個靚仔？十足十劉德華後生嗰陣呀！喍，呢啲男人先至嫁得過。唔似得果啲瘦蜢蜢嘅鬼仔咁，淨係識著住舊爛鬼白飯魚踩板。我知你唔聽你阿媽話搬咗出去住，肯定冇守身如玉啦？真係羞家。 (Will you look at this fine specimen? He looks like a young Andy Lau! Now this is a man, and the type of husband you should be pursuing. Not those skinny white boys on skateboards with dirty sneakers. I assume you're not a virgin after you moved out of home against your mother's wishes? So shameful.)

LILY: Is being a virgin part of the judging criteria for Miss Peony?

ADELINE: [*in Cantonese*] 應該要啦。 (It should be.)

LILY: Another reason why it sucks. And enough with the slut-shaming. You don't own me.

ADELINE: [*in Cantonese*] 我係你婆婆，緊係我話曬事啦。你依家聽實啊！呢啲女人全部都係好犀利嘅競爭對手—— (I'm your grandmother. Of course I own you. Now listen! You have some serious competition in these women—)

LILY: Really? Because I was nervous before but now that I'm seeing them I've never felt more confident. Old bug-eyes over there has tattooed eyebrows. Snow White is wearing knock-off Supreme from Paddy's Markets. And that woman has a Minions backpack.

ADELINE: [*in Cantonese*] 唔怪得知你冇朋友啦。你最近有冇照下鏡呀？成個四眼妹咁，著住啲穿窿牛仔褲，個頭染又到成個金毛。汪汪。 (No wonder you don't have any friends. Have you taken a look at yourself lately? Ugly glasses frames. Ripped jeans and blonde hair like a Labrador. Woof woof.)

LILY: You know what? I don't need your help! I can win this pageant on my own—

ADELINE: [*in Cantonese*] 發夢都冇咁早啦！我哋明明講好咗架！ (Like hell you will! We had a deal!)

LILY: So you can take your stupid tips, and your stupid comments, and your stupid bracelet, and you can shove it up your ghost butt—

LILY *removes the bracelet and pockets it.* ADELINE *disappears.*

Por Por?

ZHEN HUA *goes to* LILY. *His sudden appearance stuns* LILY. *How much has he heard?* ZHEN HUA *tries pinning a badge on* LILY's *top, but she dodges him.*

ZHEN HUA: [*in Mandarin*] 早安，我叫振华！我是牡丹小姐的制作人—欢迎欢迎！请问你能从现在开始把徽章带在身上吗？你是参赛者八十八号。太巧了！首先，等下你将要和评审进行面试— (Good morning, my name is Zhen Hua! I'm the producer of Miss Peony—welcome! Can you please keep this badge on you from now onwards? You are contestant number Eighty-Eight. Very fortuitous! To begin with there will be an interview with the judges—)

LILY: Whoa, whoa, whoa. That's my boob. Do fobs not understand consent?

ZHEN HUA: [*in Mandarin*] 你说甚么？ (Pardon?)

LILY: [*in Cantonese*] 有冇 …翻譯呀？ (Is there … a translator?)

ZHEN HUA: My name's Zhen Hua and I'm the producer of Miss Peony. I just wanted to say welcome, and can you please wear this badge at all times? If you have any questions please just ask.

LILY: Oh.

ZHEN HUA: And I'm sorry if I … It was an accident.

LILY: Thanks, Zhen … Hua?

ZHEN HUA: Just call me a fob. That'll be easier to remember, right?

> ZHEN HUA *leaves and* LILY *face-palms.*

SCENE 5

Casino conference hall.

Several hours later. The room has been divided into two areas: a waiting area, and an interview area. In the waiting area, MARCY *tunes an erhu as* LILY *enters, nervous and alone*—ADELINE *seemingly banished with the jade bracelet still pocketed.* MARCY *shakes Lily's hand, businesslike.*

MARCY: [*in Mandarin*] 你好。 (Hello.) My name is Marcy.

LILY: I'm Lily.

MARCY: Lily, like the flower? Have you ever tried rosewater? It has soothing effects on the skin and is good for pigmentation like yours. There's currently a two-for-one special at my family's company, Ausway, available only until November at all eight locations across New South Wales.

She hands LILY *a business card.*

LILY: [*reading*] 'Specialist exports to the mainland and beyond.'

MARCY: Where are you from?

LILY: Coffs Harbour.

MARCY: So you're not really Chinese, then. I'm from Shanghai, originally. Have you seen this instrument before?

LILY: It's an erhu, isn't it?

MARCY: [*correcting her*] Erhu.

LILY: Erhu.

MARCY: Ah! Make an 'ah' sound. You have a weak tongue. When you shop at Ausway, ask for magnesium tablets to assist with muscle strength. Then consider our competitive prices for baby formula, fish-oil capsules, and Australian-made cosmetics. Have you ever been to China?

LILY: I've only been to Hong Kong to visit extended family.

MARCY: Hong Kong is China.

A tense silence. In the interview area, we see JOY *painting calligraphy. Once she's finished,* ZHEN HUA *enters the waiting area.*

ZHEN HUA: Number Two-One-Seven? You're next.

MARCY *follows* ZHEN HUA *to the interview area. As she plays erhu,* SABRINA *enters the waiting area and sits beside* LILY. *She wears knock-off Adidas and snaps photos of the room on her phone.*

SABRINA: Can you believe that we're actually here? This is where it all started for legends like Phang Puen Chun and Yang Mei Ling. Do you think they even sat in these same chairs? I could be sitting in a past winner's chair! Hope a bit of that dust rubs off on me. I'm Sabrina, by the way!

LILY: I'm Lily. Are you an ABC too?

SABRINA: Western Sydney born and bred.

LILY: Thank god! I thought I might be the only ABC.

SABRINA: Same story, right? Selective-school kid, Chinese lessons every Saturday, TVB every night with the grandparents, barely seeing whities unless you went into the city?

LILY: Sort of. I'm sorry you had to endure all that.

SABRINA: [*confused*] Why are you sorry?

LILY: I mean, I'm not. That all sounds … awesome.

> JOY *enters the waiting area.*

SABRINA: [*to Joy*] Hi there! How was the interview?! Scary?

JOY: Not scary! But I'm sure you do better than me.

SABRINA: AGH I'M SO GEED!!!

> SABRINA *stretches, getting in the zone.* JOY *stares at* LILY, *mouth breathing.*

JOY: Candy?

LILY: Pardon?

JOY: Would you like some candy?

LILY: Um. Sure. Thanks.

> JOY *rummages in her pocket and produces a fistful of bonbons.* LILY *takes a piece from* JOY's *clenched fist.*

LILY: Still warm …

JOY: I am number Eleven. How old are you? Are you married?

LILY: I'm twenty-six. And no, I'm single.

JOY: You older than me and still alone! But don't worry. Miss Peony a good way to meet new people. That's why I enter—to find someone special. Very depress in this country by myself. But who knows, maybe I no meet anyone. Or maybe I get kick out now—I think I mess up my talent, not practise hard enough.

LILY: We needed to prepare a talent? I thought this was just a chat with the judges so they get to know us?

JOY: First, you introduce yourself. Say hello, my name is number Eleven, nice to meet you. Then you catwalk so judges can see if you fat or not fat. Last thing is you show talent, like I do calligraphy, but maybe you dance or sing or play basketball, I don't know.

> *In the interview area,* MARCY *finishes her erhu performance.* ZHEN HUA *enters the waiting area.*

ZHEN HUA: Number Sixty-Nine?

> SABRINA *jumps up and performs a short hip-hop dance in the interview area. In the waiting area,* ZHEN HUA *checks paperwork.*

[*To Joy*] Number Eleven? Could you please come with me? We need to take some reference photos.

> ZHEN HUA and JOY *leave the waiting area. The moment they're gone,* LILY *searches for the bracelet in her pocket. She finds it and slips it on.* ADELINE *appears.*

LILY: I had to bring a talent today?! And there's an interview? I thought once you filled out an entry form you were officially part of the competition!

ADELINE: [*in Cantonese*] 鬼知咩！ (Who knows?! I have no idea!)

LILY: Por Por. Please. I've already paid my first four weeks of rent in Camden. I pick up the keys next Friday!

ADELINE: [*in Cantonese*] 你又話唔駛我幫手。你話自己一個人都可以贏到牡丹小姐！ (You said you didn't need my help. You said you could win Miss Peony all on your own!)

LILY: [*reluctantly*] I was wrong.

ADELINE: [*in Cantonese*] 你話咩話？ (I didn't hear that?)

LILY: I said … I was wrong. We'll do it your way.

ADELINE: [*gleefully, in Cantonese*] 咁就啱喇！依家佢哋就篩選緊啦。佢哋年年全國各地都有幾千人報名，所以要揀番幾百個高水準嘅選手入入圍名單。只有嗰啲女仔先可以有資格參賽。我哋冇咩時間準備喇，除咗駁嘴你仲有咩叻？ (Excellent! Well right now they're culling. They get thousands of entries from around the country and need to shortlist a few hundred entrants of quality. Only those girls will get to compete. Now we don't have much time, so what are your skills besides talking back?)

LILY: I like singing.

ADELINE: [*in Cantonese*] 你識唱啲咩中文歌？ (Do you know any Chinese songs?)

LILY: [*in Cantonese*] 祝你生日快樂，祝你生日快樂 … (Happy birthday to you, happy birthday to you …)

ADELINE: [*in Cantonese*] 南無阿彌陀佛。咁背詩呢？李白首「靜夜思」你識唔識呀？ (Buddha help us. How about poetry? Do you remember 'Thoughts in the Silent Night' by Li Bai?)

LILY: Yeah. That poem is probably the only thing I liked from Chinese school.

ADELINE: [*in Cantonese*] 咁就朗誦啦。雖然簡單，但係首詩嘅意境寫得又幽美又有情懷。記住用廣東話！總之你盡力啦。實

擸到分嘅。 (Recite the poem then. It's simple, but it's beautiful and nostalgic. And speak in Cantonese! Whatever you can manage. You'll get points for that.)

ZHEN HUA returns to the waiting area.

ZHEN HUA: Number Eighty-Eight?

LILY follows ZHEN HUA into the interview area. She steps into a spotlight and squints, stumbling over her words.

LILY: [*in Cantonese*] 大家好，我係馮曉冬。今年廿六歲，住喺悉尼。身高一百六十五厘米。今日我會朗誦李白嘅《靜夜詩》：床前明月光，疑是地上霜。舉頭望明月，低頭思故鄉。多謝。 (Hello. My name is Lily Fung. I'm twenty-six years old and I live in Sydney. I'm one hundred and sixty-five centimetres tall. Today I will recite 'Thoughts in the Silent Night' by Li Bai: 'At the foot of my bed there is moonlight / It looks like frost on the ground / I raise my head to look at the moon / I lower my head and think of home.' Thank you.)

Short applause from the unseen judges. LILY bows, stunned by herself.

SCENE 6

Casino conference hall.

Shortly after. LILY returns to the waiting area to find ADELINE.

ADELINE: [*in Cantonese*] 點呀？ (How did you go?)

LILY: I did it! I can't believe I did it!

ADELINE: [*in Cantonese*] 冬冬真係叻女！但係過咗呢個環節，下次才藝表演你淨係靠背唐詩三百首唔夠家。 (Well done, Dong Dong! But you're going to need more than a four-line poem for your talent, once you get through.)

MARCY, JOY, and SABRINA enter the waiting area. LILY doesn't notice.

LILY: How are you so sure I'll make it through? What if I don't?

SABRINA: Huh?

JOY: Who are you talking to?

LILY: Nobody.

> LILY *starts slipping the bracelet off.*

ADELINE: [*in Cantonese*] 冬冬，唔好— (Dong Dong, don't—)

> LILY *pockets the bracelet and* ADELINE *disappears.*

MARCY: [*to Lily*] How was your interview?

LILY: Good, I think!

MARCY: [*through gritted teeth*] Great! If we all get in, we should stick together! There will be so many women competing in Miss Peony that we should look out for each other, like a sisterhood.

LILY: Oh. That sounds kind of nice …

JOY: I like our friendship group very much! Go sisters! [*Directed at no-one*] I'm sorry—this my first time in this building, I don't know which way to train station.

> LILY *and* SABRINA *share confused looks.*

MARCY: Ignore her. She's been talking to herself all day.

SABRINA: Maybe you guys did well—youse all spent ages in there. But they legit hated me! I chucked a phat hack and went into a muzz and then they shooed me out the door. It's probably the worst hacking they've ever seen! I want to win Miss Peony so bad, but I bet I won't even get in! I'm a loser! This was my only chance to enter before uni starts next year and I become some boring law drone. My parents reckon pageants are dumb.

LILY: Sabrina, you're not a loser.

JOY: Sabrina is your name, number Sixty-Nine?

SABRINA: [*nodding and crying*] Sixty-Nine. Nice.

> ZHEN HUA *joins them. The women jostle towards him.*

ZHEN HUA: Thanks so much for your patience today, everyone. I've got the judge's results here.

SABRINA: Just put us out of our misery man!

ZHEN HUA: Well, you must be a very talented group—

MARCY: JUST TELL US.

ZHEN HUA: Congratulations, you're all officially competing for the crown of Miss Peony!

> *Excited chitters among the women.*

LILY: What happens now?

ZHEN HUA: Over the next several days you'll be undertaking training sessions in the lead-up to the Grand Final on Saturday. The judges will be watching you closely during these sessions, which means you can be eliminated at any time. If you are eliminated, you will hear this sound.

> ZHEN HUA *gives the cue for a flat buzzer sound.*

LILY: Well that's not demoralising at all.

ZHEN HUA: Get some rest tonight because tomorrow is your first training session: DANCE!

> *The women hug each other with a lot of artificial cheer.* ZHEN HUA *begins packing up.* LILY *watches him.*

MARCY: We should celebrate with a glass of wine.

SABRINA: SHOTS!

> *The other women leave, a merry band.* LILY *hangs back and watches* ZHEN HUA. *Checks him out.*

ZHEN HUA: Can I help you with something, Lily?

LILY: Yeah. Yes. I wanted to chat to you, Zhen Hua.

ZHEN HUA: [*softening, correcting her pronunciation*] It's Zhen Hua.

LILY: I wanted to apologise for calling you a fob.

ZHEN HUA: I'm not a fob, but so what if I was? This is my community, these are my people. I've spent my whole life trying to protect them against racism—

LILY: I wasn't being racist!

ZHEN HUA: I heard you criticising those girls for wearing clothes and make-up that makes them feel comfortable. Those girls are just trying to exist—

> LILY *steps close to* ZHEN HUA.

LILY: I find it pretty ironic that a man who refers to women as 'girls' is lecturing me on feminism.

> ZHEN HUA *closes the gap.*

ZHEN HUA: Well I find it tragic that you're mocking other Chinese women when you're actually just jealous they belong here and you don't!

LILY *is stunned silent.*

Girls like you don't win Miss Peony.

> ZHEN HUA *steps back, a fleeting moment of regret. He exits, leaving* LILY *alone.*

SCENE 7

Casino conference hall.

Training session number one. SABRINA *leads the women in a dance warm-up.* JOY *is struggling but* LILY *is doing surprisingly well.* MARCY *sees this and gets slightly argy-bargy with her.*

SABRINA: Everyone feeling warm? Okay, let's bring the pace down a little!

> *The women continue dancing as* SABRINA *sidles up to* LILY.

Hey Lily, I didn't have a chance to say this yesterday when I was spiralling, but your grandmother was amazing. I've seen all the pageants she competed in—at least, the ones they uploaded to YouTube. I recognised you the moment we met because you look just like her, but I didn't want to fangirl and make it weird. The fan dance Adeline Yu performed at Miss Hong Kong 1957 is the stuff of legends.

MARCY: [*to Lily*] ADELINE YU IS YOUR GRANDMOTHER?

JOY: [*to no-one*] Hmm difficult to choose but I think Shih Tzu my favourite dog breed because they so soft and their name sound like rude word in English! [*To the women*] Sorry. Who is Adeline Yu?

SABRINA: Only the most famous beauty queen in Hong Kong! She was one of the founders of Miss Peony in Australia. She wanted to uphold our culture among the Chinese Australian diaspora and create a community where we could all feel welcome.

LILY: Yeah, she did a great job of that. What a welcoming community and what a wonderful pageant.

JOY: Your family famous, Lily.

MARCY: It's an unfair advantage. What else are you keeping from us? Have you had liposuction? Breast augmentation? I regret offering you discounts at all eight Ausway locations across New South Wales.

SABRINA: I got implants at the start of this year! That was after my jaw shaving, skin bleaching … and I've gotten Botox a few times.

JOY: Preventative Botox. Very good.

LILY: But isn't the winner of Miss Peony supposed to be the woman who most 'exemplifies Chinese values in modern Australia'? Like, I don't know what the hell those values are, but this competition's not just about looks, right?

The other women burst out laughing.

JOY: We still women, Lily! Oh, you so funny.

LILY: So Miss Peony is just about beauty?

MARCY: Of course not!

SABRINA: The rules state that you have to be at least bilingual …

MARCY: And you must embody traditional Chinese values.

LILY: But what does that even mean! 'Chinese values' are different in each family, each country. And what if you're only Chinese in some ways?

SABRINA: [*thinking*] Hmm, true … Lee Hoe Yee won last year because she had the best talent but she couldn't even count to ten in Mando. But she was still super pretty! And she had double-Ds.

JOY: Traditionally, Chinese girls are flat-chested.

LILY: But not all of them are! And what if you're not pretty but you're a bigshot in the community? Could you still win? What about all of those grey areas? Doesn't the criteria seem conflicted to you?

MARCY: [*pointedly*] If you're so confused by Miss Peony, why didn't you ask your grandmother about it?

They're interrupted by the elimination buzzer sounding twice in the next room. A beat, and then one more buzzer sounds. ZHEN HUA *enters and stretches before the women, arse in the air.* LILY *stares.*

SABRINA: Don't get dickmatised, Lily. Focus!

JOY: What is dickmatise?

SABRINA: When you're hypnotised by the D.

LILY: I'm not dickmatised! Chinese guys aren't my type.

SABRINA: Really? I reckon Zhen Hua's even hotter than my first boyfriend Kenny who shit himself eating ten hot dogs at Harry's de Wheels after our formal.

MARCY: No doubt the other contestants are trying to sleep their way to the top with him. Lily, your skin looks flushed. Maybe you need some aloe vera gel—I can get you some from Ausway at wholesale price.

LILY: I'm fine, Marcy.

SABRINA: Don't you think Zhen Hua's hot, Joy?

JOY: [*in Mandarin*] 客觀來講他是挺帥的。可是我是蕾絲邊，對他一點感覺也沒有。 (Objectively he's handsome. But I'm a lesbian. He stirs nothing in me.)

> MARCY *has a coughing fit upon hearing this.*

LILY: [t*o Sabrina*] What did Joy say?

SABRINA: My Mando's not fluent but I think she said she's gay.

> MARCY *continues coughing.*

LILY: Marcy, your skin looks flushed. Maybe you need some aloe vera.

ZHEN HUA: All right! I hope everyone's warmed up and ready for some D-A-N-C-I-N-G! I trust you all watched the choreography I sent last night? There's another group arriving soon so we'll jump straight into the routine.

> ZHEN HUA *blasts the music—something disco and daggy like 'Rhythm Is a Dancer'.*

FIVE, SIX, SEVEN, EIGHT!

> ZHEN HUA *and the women dance. While they're distracted,* LILY *steps away and puts the jade bracelet on.* ADELINE *appears.*

ADELINE: [*in Cantonese*] 點解你唔跟住佢哋跳啊？冬冬，你唔遵守規則會俾人踢出局㗎！ (Why aren't you dancing with the rest of them? You'll be eliminated if you don't follow instructions, Dong Dong!)

LILY: Por Por, why did you help found Miss Peony?

ADELINE: [*in Cantonese*] 你講咩啊？你依家專心啲跳舞啦！ (What are you talking about? You should be focusing on dancing right now!)

LILY: The judging criteria is so conflicted.

ADELINE: [*in Cantonese*] 邊度係咧。凡事都有啱同錯嘅做法，你依家就做錯緊呀！ (No it's not. There is a right and a wrong way of doing things, and right now you are doing the wrong thing!)

LILY: So what is the right thing? How do you actually win Miss Peony? What makes someone Chinese enough to wear the crown?

ADELINE: [*in Cantonese*] 我遲啲會話俾你知㗎喇。今晚啦。但係依家你一定要跳呀！唔該你喇！ (I will show you. Tonight. But please! Right now you have to dance!)

> LILY *rejoins the formation but she's slightly out of step.*

ZHEN HUA: Come on, Lily! Keep up!

SCENE 8

Lily's hotel room.

That evening. ADELINE *performs her fan dance. She is elegant and poised.* LILY *enters smoking a cigarette.* ADELINE *snatches it from her mouth and stubs it.*

LILY: Hey!

ADELINE: [*in Cantonese*] 依家婆婆嘅牡丹小姐地獄式訓練正式開始。你咪問過我點樣先可以贏到牡丹小姐嘅？ 牡丹小姐象徵住東方女性所有嘅特質—弱質纖纖得嚟講野又輕聲細語，同埋要代表住華人自豪嘅價值觀。 (Now we begin Por Por's Miss Peony bootcamp. You asked me what it takes to win Miss Peony? Miss Peony is the embodiment of Chinese femininity—delicate, soft-spoken, and a proud representative of Chinese values.)

LILY: And what exactly are those values?

ADELINE: [*in Cantonese*] 係咪真係要我解釋俾你聽呀？ (Do I really have to explain?)

LILY: I think you can't explain because you don't actually know. Maybe there are timeless Chinese values like stoicism and filial piety, but modern Chinese values are fluid and relative.

ADELINE: [*in Cantonese*] 冇入過大學，讀得書少，仲喺度牙擦擦。 (You sure talk a lot for someone who didn't go to university.)

LILY: Do you have an answer?

ADELINE: [*in Cantonese*] 我排曬好次序。決賽嘅才藝表演就跳我嘅扇子舞。實冧死啲評判呀。 (I have an order. Perform my fan dance for your talent at the Grand Final. It's a sure-fire bet for the judges.)

LILY: I don't have time to learn that routine. And you haven't answered my question!

ADELINE: [*in Cantonese*] 你都未試過跳我嘅扇子舞。 (Well you haven't tried my fan dance.)

LILY: Shouldn't I perform something that I'm actually good at? I've got a party trick, actually. I can do a Gollum voice. 'Sneaky little Hobbitses! Wicked. Tricksy. False. Gollum!'

ADELINE: [*in Cantonese*] Gollum係咩呀？ (What is a Gollum?)

LILY: He's from *Lord of the Rings*!

ADELINE: [*in Cantonese*] 我唔該你停手啊，如果唔係我成世都塞喺呢度，本來我依家可以上天堂同張國榮嚟個法式濕吻。 (I'm begging you to stop or I'll be stuck here forever when I could be in heaven right now kissing Leslie Cheung.)

LILY: Leslie Cheung was gay.

ADELINE: [*in Cantonese*] 嘥鬼曬。 (What a waste.)

LILY: Por Por, that's homophobic. What if I sing something? I've got some good karaoke tracks up my sleeve.

LILY *sings 'Buses and Trains' by Bachelor Girl.*

ADELINE: [*in Cantonese*] 俾巴士剷過？俾火車撞？大吉利是。唔好啦。咪再講埋你啲鬼仔垃圾野。快啲整杯咖啡俾你自己飲喇—你今晚睇嚟都係要通頂學我啲舞步喇。呢個扇子舞跳跳下，就幫你跳到去倫敦機場啦。啱啦，俾心機咁練習，攞咗個皇冠，跟著「卜」一聲你婆婆就會消失家啦。 (Walked under a bus? Got hit by a train? Go touch some wood right now. No. None of your Western rubbish. Go make yourself some coffee—you'll be burning the midnight oil learning my choreography. This fan dance will be your one-way ticket to Heathrow Airport. Yes. Practise hard, win the crown, and poof!—your meddling Por Por will disappear.)

LILY: So I just need to learn the dance?

ADELINE: [*in Cantonese*] 練下舞，執下你個樣。聽日你有媒體訓練，個個實望實你家。都唔知你染到成頭金毛果陣諗咩嘅 … (Learn the dance and change your look. Tomorrow you've got media training so all eyes will be on you. I don't know what you were thinking with this blonde hair …)

LILY: I'm not changing myself for a stupid pageant. I like my look!

ADELINE: [*in Cantonese*] 呢個先係問題呀。你究竟想唔想贏牡丹小姐家？ (That's the problem. Do you want to win Miss Peony or not?)

LILY: Just … don't overdo it.

> *A montage of* ADELINE *fixing* LILY*'s clothes and make-up. She removes* LILY*'s glasses and covers her tattoos. Finally—*LILY*'s blonde hair. What are they going to do about it?* ADELINE *presents a bottle of black hair dye and* LILY *groans.*

SCENE 9

Casino conference hall.

Training session number two. MARCY, SABRINA *and* JOY *stand before a microphone as* ZHEN HUA *checks their names off. In the next room, the elimination buzzer is sounding. More contestants are being eliminated.* SABRINA *fiddles, nervous.* MARCY *and* JOY *accidentally touch hands and then step apart from each other—a moment of awkward, sexual tension.*

SABRINA: [*to Marcy*] Have you been counting the buzzers?

MARCY: [*nodding*] They must be down to the top twenty now.

SABRINA: That was fast.

ZHEN HUA: Number Two-One-Seven, Sixty-Nine, Eleven. Where's Eighty-Eight?

JOY: [*to no-one*] Yes I agree, black sesame in egg rolls very tasty, but when I cook I make mine without seeds in case people allergic to nuts.

ZHEN HUA: We're running behind schedule …

SABRINA: Should we wait a bit longer for Lily?

MARCY: Why should we be punished for her tardiness?

ZHEN HUA: We may as well get started … Now, some general interview tips that might be helpful—eye contact is important. So is being personal with your answers. Show us who you are and what makes you unique. And try to avoid saying 'um' and 'ah'. So, number Sixty-Nine—

SABRINA: Um.

ZHEN HUA: You're the youngest competitor among our finalists. Do you think your age serves as an advantage or disadvantage?

SABRINA: Ah—

ZHEN HUA: Remember my tips?

SABRINA: Yeah, cool, sorry. [*in Cantonese*] 對我嚟講年齡只係一個數字。Natalie Kwok喺一九九八年奪得牡丹小姐冠軍嘅時候都只係十九歲。我特登用我去WSU讀法律同埋商務雙學位之前空出嚟嘅時間嚟到參加牡丹小姐，所以我認為我俾同齡人更加有野心、更加有專注力。但係我亦都覺得好榮幸可以成為今屆最後生嘅參賽者，我會繼續努力。 (To me age is just a number. Natalie Kwok was just nineteen when she won Miss Peony in 1998. I'm dedicating my gap year to competing in Miss Peony before undertaking a dual law and commerce degree at WSU, so I believe that I'm more ambitious and focused than many people my age. But I do feel very humbled being the youngest contestant and wish to keep learning.)

ZHEN HUA: That was great, Sabrina. Adding in a bit of pageant trivia was a nice touch too. On to number Eleven—

He's interrupted by LILY *entering. She looks like a younger version of* ADELINE: *a bombshell with black hair and red lipstick.* ZHEN HUA *stops in his tracks.*

LILY: Sorry I'm late.

SABRINA: LILY OH MY GOD.

MARCY: There should be a penalty for lateness.

JOY: Lily, you so beautiful!

SABRINA: I love your outfit. I'm just wearing this old thing.

JOY: Is your dress silk? Sexy fabric!

LILY: Do you really think so?

MARCY: Yes. How many times do you need to hear it? You were ugly before and now you're beautiful.

LILY: Thanks?

ZHEN HUA: [*flustered*] Yep, yep, can we all please focus on the task at hand here which is media training and not gawking! Lily was late so it doesn't matter if she looks gorgeous because I'm a professional and this is my job and I do it well, and looks aren't everything you know, especially if she's rude but also unexpectedly pretty kind, so I don't know why you all keep going on about it instead of just letting us get on with the session!

The women stare at ZHEN HUA. ZHEN HUA *and* LILY *lock eyes.*

LILY: You think I'm gorgeous?

ZHEN HUA: Number Eleven!

JOY: Greetings.

ZHEN HUA: How would you respond to critics who view pageants as superficial or shallow?

JOY: [*in Mandarin*] 我的博士論文《自治與表達對比論》探討了女權主義者如何在臺灣把個人原則的概念和在這個父權和資本主義制度下的經濟體系中建立的「選擇」來調解自身潛意識內的消費欲望。控制的盡頭到底在哪，而自治的源頭從何開始呢？我們的欲望並沒有對與錯之分。可是，我們必須意識到它們的存在，並經常考察它們。個人而言，我非常享受挑戰牡丹小姐。這場競賽也提醒了我們的社區是有多麼優美和多元化的。謝謝。 (My postdoctoral exegesis 'Autonomy versus Expression' interrogates how feminists in Taiwan reconcile their own unconscious consumer desires with the concept of personal agency and 'choice' in a patriarchal and capitalist economic system. Where does control end and where does autonomy begin? Our desires are neither correct nor incorrect. However we must be conscious of their existence and question them regularly. Personally, I've enjoyed being challenged by Miss Peony. This competition has also been a reminder of how beautiful and diverse our peoples are. Thank you.)

A long beat as everyone recovers from the shock of JOY *speaking.*

LILY: I didn't understand a word of that but it sounded impressive.

ZHEN HUA: Great work, Joy. Just remember to make eye contact.

SABRINA: Who needs eye contact when you're that much of a brainiac! Your exegesis sounds super-interesting, Joy.

MARCY: [*in Mandarin*] 可能你觉得这种普遍台湾人的思维很有趣吧。整天「我、我、我」。从来都不为群体，或者大众利益着想。我反对这种顽固的个人主义。 (If you find that typical Taiwanese mentality interesting. Always 'me, me, me'. Never about the collective or what will benefit the greater good. I reject pig-headed individualism.)

JOY: [*in Mandarin*] 所以你看上去過得真好啊。 (And you seem so content as a result.)

MARCY: [*in Mandarin*] 我很开心。我的生活很幸福。 (I lead a happy life. I'm very happy.)

ZHEN HUA: Marcy, please. Now Two-One-Seven, you're a businesswoman. What are you learning from Miss Peony that you haven't encountered in your professional life?

MARCY: [*in Mandarin*] 其实俩者之间的相似比差异更多。这两个岗位都需要与人沟通的技能和一股支持澳华社区的热诚。每天我和家人都在透过我们的公司Ausway一心一意为人民服务，这包括了在遍布于新州的八个地方提供优质的产品，出口到内陆甚至更广。 (There are more similarities than differences. Both roles require people skills and a passion for supporting the Chinese-Australian community. Every day my family and I are dedicated to serving our people through our company, Ausway, which provides quality exports to the mainland and beyond through eight locations across New South Wales.)

JOY: [*in Mandarin*] 你還真是廢話連篇呢。 (You sound like a broken record.)

MARCY: [*in Mandarin*] 你再说一次。 (SAY THAT AGAIN.)

> ZHEN HUA *steps in before a fight breaks out.*

ZHEN HUA: Thank you Marcy! Just remember what I said about showing the judges who you are. They want to get to know you, not your family's store. And finally, number Eighty-Eight. You impressed the judges in your interview. Can you tell us about what Li Bai's poem means to you?

LILY: [*in Cantonese*] 床前明月光，疑是地上霜。舉頭望明月，低頭思故鄉。李白呢一首詩對我嚟講好重要，因為 … ('At the foot of my bed there is moonlight / It looks like frost on the ground / I raise my head to look at the moon / I lower my head and think of home.' Li Bai's poem is important to me because …) What's the word for 'comforting'? Maybe one of my friends could help?

> LILY *looks to the other women for assistance but they all avert their gaze.*

Could you please give me a moment? I … need to fix my contact lenses.

MARCY: Ah! None of us got to pause! Penalise her! Or are you giving her preferential treatment because you think she's cute?

JOY: [*in Mandarin*] Marcy，放輕鬆。 (Relax, Marcy.)

MARCY: [*in Mandarin*] 你别对我指指点点！ (Don't you tell me what to do!)

In a private corner, LILY *puts the jade bracelet on and* ADELINE *appears.*

LILY: Please help me! I sound like a toddler.

ADELINE: [*in Cantonese*] 都話一早搵我幫手啦！(You should have asked for me earlier!)

ADELINE possesses LILY, *who strides back to the microphone with confidence.*

LILY: [*in Cantonese*] 多謝你嘅問題。我婆婆係語言學校教識我呢一首詩。未來有朝一日我都希望可以教識俾我嘅子孫，將余玲玲嘅傳奇傳承落去。 (Thank you for your question. My grandmother taught me that poem at Chinese school. One day I hope to teach it to my own grandchildren so that I may continue the legacy of the great Adeline Yu.)

SABRINA: Lily, you could speak fluent Canto this whole time? Why would you keep that from us?

ADELINE possesses SABRINA *who begins barking like a dog.*

MARCY: Why did you lie about being Adeline Yu's granddaughter?

ADELINE possesses MARCY *who begins squawking like a chicken.*

JOY: And then how you become pretty? What else you hiding, Lily?

ADELINE possesses JOY *who goes cross-eyed and hops around on one leg.*

ZHEN HUA: What is going on? Are you all pranking me?

Despite herself, LILY *is amused by* ADELINE'*s antics. They share a private giggle before* LILY *removes the bracelet and* ADELINE *disappears. The other women recover immediately.*

LILY: [*to Zhen Hua*] I think everyone's exhausted! None of us have been eating or sleeping properly since the competition started and the eliminations have had everyone stressed.

ZHEN HUA looks at the other women, who all look slightly dazed.

ZHEN HUA: We've got the charity session tomorrow. Let's quickly take some press shots and then everyone should get some rest. Go see the medic if you need to. I'll go first. Sabrina, I think you may have bitten me …

ZHEN HUA *leaves. The women pose for photographs.*

LILY: So much for the sisterhood. The second I struggled you all let me tank because—

MARCY: Lily this is a competition at the end of the day—

LILY: I wasn't finished speaking—

SABRINA: [*in Cantonese*] 你收收埋埋扮冇料咁仲好講—(And you're not one to talk considering you hid all of your abilities from us—)

LILY: Can you let me speak—

JOY: [*in Mandarin*] 你欺騙了大家，我們還要怎麼做姊妹呢？ (How can we be sisters if you lie to us?)

LILY: Shut up! Just shut up and let me talk, okay?! That's all you people do—interrupt, and push in, and act two-faced so you can get ahead in life! All you care about is status and money and … tacky clothes with far too many sequins on them! People like you are the whole reason why the rest of the world hates us! You're so obsessed with this pageant when it's actually just bullshit. Because if you guys are the best examples of what it means to be Chinese then I'd rather be dead.

MARCY *storms out.*

I didn't mean that. Joy? Sabrina?

JOY *and* SABRINA *storm out, leaving* LILY *alone.*

SCENE 10

Casino conference hall.

Training session number three. ZHEN HUA *enters and raises a champagne glass. Nearby,* SABRINA *and* MARCY *try selling roses to audience members.*

ZHEN HUA: Hello and good evening! I hope you're all enjoying the cocktails and canapés. Before the night gets away from us, I'd like to raise a glass to you—esteemed members of the Miss Peony extended family. Thank you all for your continued financial support. Particularly from our platinum sponsor, Mr Kenneth Lam, without whom Miss Peony would not exist. As you know, we're here for our ever-popular charity event, where the contestants have been competing to sell the most roses. Their prize? A coveted spot in our top twelve! Can you believe by this time tomorrow evening we'll have crowned our new Miss Peony? Thank you, and please enjoy the dance floor!

>LILY *enters and approaches* MARCY *and* JOY.

LILY: Hi.

>*They ignore her.*

Marcy?

MARCY: Stick to your side of the room.

LILY: Sabrina?

SABRINA: Don't waste your breath.

LILY: Marcy, I'm sorry. Sabrina, I know you must be so disappointed in me. And Joy—where's Joy?

SABRINA: Talking to Ken Lam. They've been gone for ages. Why didn't he choose to talk to me?

MARCY: What does he see in Joy, anyway? Yes, she's intelligent and funny, and she has a very cute dimple in her left cheek when she laughs at a joke you make …

LILY: Shouldn't Joy be out here with us?

MARCY: Why do you care?

>*They turn their backs on* LILY. LILY *goes to* ZHEN HUA.

LILY: Hey, have you seen Joy and Ken Lam? They've been missing for a while.

ZHEN HUA: Sorry Lily, I'm working. Ah! Mrs Chen! How are Bam Bam and Bobbi? They're such handsome poodles!

>ZHEN HUA *goes to speak to an audience member ('Mrs Chen') but is interrupted by the loud voices of* KEN LAM *and* JOY.

KEN LAM: [*offstage, in Cantonese*] 八婆，停手呀！豈有此理居然咁樣對長輩！ (Get off me, you bitch! How dare you treat an old man like this!)

JOY: [*offstage, in Mandarin*] 你這個令人作惡的變態，還有更多讓你嘗嘗呢！ (THERE'S PLENTY MORE WHERE THAT CAME FROM YOU DISGUSTING CREEP!)

>*Suddenly,* JOY *appears looking dishevelled. Offstage, a loud yell from* KEN LAM.

ZHEN HUA: Mr Lam!!!

>	ZHEN HUA *exits, looking for Ken Lam.*

LILY: Joy! Are you okay?!

JOY: He come into toilet. Pull out penis, tell me to touch.

MARCY: [*in Mandarin*] 那个混蛋！ (THAT BASTARD!)

>	MARCY *tries to chase after Ken Lam but* SABRINA *restrains her.*

[*In Mandarin*] 他没强迫你干甚么吧，有吗？ (He didn't make you do anything, did he?)

JOY: [*in Mandarin*] 沒有，我把他打跑了。 (No, I fought him off.)

>	ZHEN HUA *returns, looking pale.*

ZHEN HUA: Ken Lam's gone. What happened?

LILY: He tried to assault Joy in the toilets!

ZHEN HUA: What?! Oh my god!

LILY: Aren't you going to do something?

ZHEN HUA: I … Well … How do we know for sure?

LILY: You don't believe her.

ZHEN HUA: There weren't any witnesses and I'm just trying to be balanced!

JOY: I WAS WITNESS! Saw everything with my own two eyes! Why would I make up? Why I want to ruin Miss Peony when everyone work so hard?

MARCY: To men, women are always wrong.

ZHEN HUA: Marcy, I didn't say that! And aren't you being kind of sexist towards men with that generalisation?

SABRINA: Dude. I wouldn't go there.

JOY: SEXIST TOWARDS MEN? SEXISM CANNOT EXIST AGAINST MEN WHEN THEY ARE THE GOVERNING FORCE IN A PATRIARCHAL SOCIAL SYSTEM.

>	JOY *storms out.* MARCY *and* SABRINA *follow her.*

ZHEN HUA: What do you expect me to do? I'm kind of caught between a rock and a hard place here!

LILY: You're so self-righteous when it comes to race but you're being wilfully blind when it comes to gender. If you actually cared about the Chinese community as much as you say you do, you'd fight for the most vulnerable people in it. Look at yourself: you're a grown man running a beauty pageant. Who do you think you are? Donald Trump? [*Echoing Zhen Hua*] Men like you shouldn't run Miss Peony.

She exits, leaving a contrite ZHEN HUA *behind.*

SCENE 11

A hot pot restaurant.

Later that evening. The women sit in silence, solemn. LILY *stirs the hotpot and serves everyone, trying to lighten the mood.*

LILY: More fish?

MARCY: [*to Joy, in Mandarin*] 你別再想着振华了，他就是个傻逼。 (Don't worry about Zhen Hua. He's a fool.)

JOY: [*in Mandarin*] 說出來太羞恥了，但是我當時很害怕。 (I'm ashamed to say this, but I was scared.)

MARCY: [*in Mandarin*] 这事是很可怕！ (It WAS scary!)

JOY: I never scare of Ken Lam. I scare of myself because I felt like I have enough rage to hurt him. Maybe even kill him. All of my anger towards men almost spill over, cause a mess. Does that make me evil?

LILY: Evil? It makes you relatable!

JOY: [*in Mandarin*] 你知道他把小弟弟拿出來的時候我做了甚麼嗎？我歎氣了，因為我已經對男人這樣的行為習以為常。然後我就生我自己的氣，因為我不應該習慣它。有時候我想交男朋友也只是為了讓其他男人放過我。如果我屬於另一個男人，至少他們會尊重他的「財產」。 (Do you know what I did when he pulled out his dick? I sighed, because I am so used to that kind of behaviour from men. And then I was angry because I shouldn't have to be used to it. Sometimes I just want to get a boyfriend so other men will finally leave me alone. If I belong to another man, at least they will respect his 'property'.)

SABRINA: Oh Joy. You don't believe that.

LILY: What'd she say?

SABRINA: She wants a beard, but even that won't stop guys from being gross scumbags.

MARCY: [*in Mandarin*] 她说的对。社会教导男人从小厌女。如果你比他们更聪明、收入更高，即使是所谓的「好男人」都

会觉得被精神阉割。 (She's right. Society teaches men to hate women from a young age. Even the so-called 'nice guys' may feel emasculated if you're more intelligent than them or earn a higher salary.)

LILY: I had one customer at work wearing a 'The Future is Female' shirt kiss me at a buck's night, tongue and everything. It wasn't even the kiss that disturbed me. It was his attitude. The sense of entitlement.

SABRINA: Once I had a guy peeping tom me in the Market City Timezone toilets and I called the police but it took them ages—ACAB—so the guy got away and it never got resolved. In the end I was so freaked out I had to stop going to Timezone and give my VIP membership card to my nephew. He used all my points on a Sonic backpack. It was terrible. So it's understandable why you're so angry, Joy.

JOY: [*in Mandarin*] 可能是我自己拿來的。我堂堂一名性別研究學者，居然來參加選美比賽！我到底在幹甚麼？我應該退賽。 (Maybe I brought this upon myself. I'm an academic in gender studies taking part in a beauty pageant! What am I doing? I should quit.)

SABRINA: Don't quit, Joy!

LILY: Miss Peony needs you, Joy. What you did was inspiring. You're all inspiring. Forget about Zhen Hua and—and have some more quail eggs instead!

JOY: Thank you, Lily. For your words, and for your eggs.

MARCY: We're 'inspiring' are we? I thought you'd rather be dead than be like us.

LILY: I'm sorry. I can't believe I said that.

SABRINA: I'm sorry too, guys. I promised myself I wouldn't be bitchy and competitive when I entered because that's not who I am. I'm just heaps passionate because the women in Miss Peony were my heroes growing up. They were the first people I saw on TV who looked like me and were winning at life instead of, you know, being investigated on *A Current Affair* and stuff. I entered because I was like, whoa, it'd be awesome to be that person for someone else one day. Be a role model for the other ABCs out there. And on an international stage in Beijing! Getting to meet all the other Miss Peony winners from around the world.

JOY: Very good, Sabrina. On hard days like this, good to remind myself why I enter Miss Peony: to find a loving partner.

>   MARCY *spits out her tea.*

So many beautiful women competing and watching—better than dating app. Maybe I can find best friend. Then hopefully fall in love. I can't have that at home. Even though Taiwan make gay people legal, still my parents no accept. Still punishing me.

MARCY: I have the opposite problem. My parents gave me everything and now it's my turn to repay them. My brother ran our company into the ground. I'm the one with the business smarts but he has too much pride to let me take over. I entered Miss Peony to save Ausway; we need the prize money. If sales don't improve, we will lose all eight locations across New South Wales and have to file for bankruptcy. Please don't tell anyone.

SABRINA: Oh Marcy, I'm so sorry! My parents love buying bulk paw paw ointment from Ausway! Why did you enter, Lily?

LILY: I entered for my grandmother. And once the pageant is finished, I'll move to London.

JOY: Why you go to England? You want to be colonise again?

LILY: I guess the destination never mattered. I'm more drawn to the idea of starting anew.

MARCY: Trust me as a business owner when I say that starting anew can be overrated. Sometimes it's more worthwhile to focus on fixing what you already have.

JOY: Excuse me. I have to go weewee.

>   JOY *exits.*

LILY: I haven't eaten hot pot since I was a kid. This has been really nice.

SABRINA: Hot pot is the best! But make sure you always go with your Chinese friends 'cause whenever I go with whities they're like, 'So you have to cook your own food?' It's so frustrating. I just want to drink my watermelon juice in peace.

LILY: I don't have many white friends. Or Chinese friends for that matter. I've always kind of been a lone ranger.

MARCY: Oh Lily, that's sad.

LILY: I'm fine! I'm always busy with work. And I like to read. I just finished reading *Jane Eyre*.

SABRINA: That whole book is about lonely women.

LILY: Oh.

SABRINA: Here! Have some more juice! [*Filling everyone's cups*] We should toast to—to making friends! And to making the top twelve and persisting despite all the shit that went down. I can't believe Miss Peony ends tomorrow night.

> *They raise their glasses.*

LILY: Wait. Where did Joy go?

SABRINA: To the toilet. Good on her. Exposure therapy.

MARCY: No, she did not go to the toilet. She went to pay!

> JOY *returns to the table and smugly takes a seat.*

[*In Mandarin*] 你现在是认真的吗！(Are you serious right now?!)

JOY: [*in Mandarin*] 我來，我請客！(My shout, my shout!)

SABRINA: [*in Cantonese*] 唔得呀，傻婆！我請呀！ (No, you stupid cow! I'm paying!)

MARCY: [*in Mandarin*] 我来付。 (I AM PAYING.)

SABRINA: [*to Joy, in Cantonese*] 我會叫佢哋退返你張咭！(I'll make them refund your card!)

MARCY: [*in Mandarin*] 把帐单给我，不然— (Give me the bill or—)

JOY: [*in Mandarin*] 不然怎樣？(Or what?)

MARCY: [*in Mandarin*] 不然我会咀咒你！ (Or I'll wish you bad luck!)

SABRINA: [*in Cantonese*] 我會係你面前放屁！(I'll fart in your face!)

MARCY: [*in Mandarin*] 我会绊倒你！(I'll trip you over!)

SABRINA: [*in Cantonese*] 我會燒窿你隻手！(I'll give you an arm burn!)

MARCY: [*in Mandarin*] 我会揍你！(I'll punch you!)

SABRINA: [*in Cantonese*] 我會毒死你！(I'll poison you!)

MARCY: [*in Mandarin*] 我会打断你的腿！(I'll break your leg!)

SABRINA: [*in Cantonese*] 我會界爛你嘅車胎！(I'll slash your tyres!)

MARCY: [*in Mandarin*] 我会在你家人熟睡的时候闯进你的家，切开他们的喉咙，直到他们被自己流的血窒息而亡。 (I WILL BREAK INTO YOUR HOUSE WHILE YOUR FAMILY IS SLEEPING AND SLIT THEIR THROATS UNTIL THEY DROWN TO DEATH CHOKING ON THEIR OWN BLOOD.)

SABRINA: Marcy. What is wrong with you?

MARCY: I am older than you both! It's my responsibility.

SABRINA: I'm the youngest! I should be shouting!

LILY: Well, I'm the eldest here. How about we just split the bill equally between us all?

    The other women fall silent, disturbed.

JOY: You from Coffs Harbour.

LILY: What's that got to do with anything?

JOY: At Coffs Harbour they have Big Banana. That's you.

SABRINA: I'm an ABC too but you're like, next level, man.

MARCY: But it's okay. We still like you.

LILY: Really?

SABRINA: I'm heaps glad we got to become friends before you move away! My parents aren't gonna believe I met Adeline Yu's granddaughter. I'm still pinching myself.

    The women gather their things to leave. LILY *hangs back and touches her jade bracelet.*

JOY: Lily? We going to get dessert.

LILY: You go. I should get some beauty sleep for the ceremony tomorrow.

SCENE 12

Lily's hotel room.

Late that evening. LILY *slips on her jade bracelet and* ADELINE *appears.*

LILY: Por Por, I'm sorry it's been so long! I actually kind of missed (you) —!

ADELINE: [*in Cantonese*] 我哋爭少少咋，冬冬！你有冇勤力練我排嘅扇子舞呀？ (We're getting so close, Dong Dong! Have you been practising my fan dance choreography?) [*Sniffing*] 你最近食過煙呀？ (And have you been smoking?)

LILY: [*lying*] No. And I haven't had time to practise.

ADELINE: [*in Cantonese*] 點解呀？我哋冇時間啦喎！ (Why? We're running out of time!)

LILY: I was out at dinner with the other contestants and they're all so cool and funny and strong. Joy did the right thing standing up against Ken Lam.

ADELINE: [*in Cantonese*] 林百祥做乜事啊？ (What happened with Ken Lam?)

LILY: Joy fought back after he exposed his dick to her. He left the charity event.

ADELINE: [*in Cantonese*] 蠢材。 (Stupid girl.)

LILY: What?

ADELINE: [*in Cantonese*] 我話佢真係蠢啊！林百祥不嬲都出名鹹濕㗎啦。當初我參選嗰陣佢已經喺香港做選美評判啦。佢曾經仲會靜雞雞入嚟我哋更衣室借啲意博懵，講埋嘥啲核突嘢，仲迫啲女仔陪佢上床呀。我哋嗰陣咪又係啞巴食黃連、繼續比賽。你個朋友唔應該出聲。 (I said she's a stupid girl! Kenneth Lam has had a reputation for years. He was a judge in Hong Kong pageants when I was still competing. He would sneak into change rooms and touch us, say disgusting things, pressured some girls into sleeping with him. We sucked it up and carried on. It was wrong of your friend to say something.)

LILY: It was wrong of Ken Lam. The pageant is better off without him!

ADELINE: [*in Cantonese*] 冇林百祥啲錢未來仲邊度會有選美啊！ (Without Ken Lam's money there will be no future pageants!)

LILY: So what if the pageant dies out? As long as I win Miss Peony tomorrow night, you'll be free.

ADELINE: [*in Cantonese*] 梗係重要喇！牡丹小姐係我嘅心血，點可以後繼無人！ (Of course it matters! Miss Peony is my legacy!)

LILY: Hello?! Your legacy is standing right here! I'm your flesh and blood!

ADELINE: [*in Cantonese*] 你？你冇樣嘢似我。又唔識講又唔識煮，更加唔識收埋把口。你從來都冇試過做一個華人。 (You? You're nothing like me. Can't speak the language. Can't cook the food. Can't hold your tongue. You have never even tried to be Chinese.)

LILY: I have tried, actually. I tried really freaking hard but it was never good enough for you! I got Cantonese lessons but you and everyone else at Chinese school laughed at my accent. I learnt how to write but you said there's no point because my strokes were in the wrong order. I use chopsticks but apparently, I don't hold them correctly! I sat the UMAT but my score wasn't good enough for the med school you wanted. You begged me to be financially secure but you hate my job at the bar—

ADELINE: [*in Cantonese*] 管理酒吧唔係一個正經華人女仔會做嘅
嘢！就算你唔去讀醫，你都至少應該走去做律師或者會計
啦！ (Managing a bar isn't a respectable job for a Chinese girl!
And if you weren't going to do medicine you should have at least
done law or accounting!)

LILY: When am I ever going to be enough for you?

ADELINE: [*in Cantonese*] 你幾時先可以似番個真真正正嘅華人啊！
(When you act properly Chinese!)

LILY: What does that even mean?! Do you even know? Because if
I don't win Miss Peony tomorrow night, it's going to be your fault!

ADELINE: [*in Cantonese*] 我嘅錯？明明就係你衰咗點會係我嘅錯
呀？你依家為咗嗌贏交就由得你婆婆以後做隻孤魂嘢鬼咁
慘？你真係冇鬼用啊！阻住個地球轉！我以後無面再叫你做
我孫女啦！ (My fault? My fault when you are the failure? You
would allow your own grandmother to suffer in purgatory for the
sake of winning an argument right now? You're useless! A waste of
space! I'm ashamed to call you my granddaughter!)

LILY: Then fuck off!

　　　LILY *smashes the bracelet and* ADELINE *disappears.*

ACT TWO

Note: Act Two occurs over the course of one evening.

SCENE 13

Casino confererence hall.

The next evening. It's the pageant Grand Final. Spotlights sweep the stage as the women perform a slick opening dance routine. They exit as ZHEN HUA *enters in a dazzling suit.*

ZHEN HUA: [*in Mandarin*] 大家晚上好，欢迎来到悉尼星河赌场现场直播的牡丹小姐总决赛。我是今晚的大会主持，吴振华。 (Hello and welcome to the Miss Peony Grand Final, televised live from Galaxies Casino in Sydney! My name is Wu Zhen Hua, your host for this evening.) Over the past five days, hundreds of Chinese women from around Australia have been competing for the title of Miss Peony. It's been a gruelling elimination process that has tested our contestants' mental and physical prowess, and given our esteemed judges much food for thought! Please join me in welcoming our judges now: Bessie Li, star of the drama, *Help! My Husband is a Monkey!*; Alvin To, COO of Apex, Hurstville's leading luxury-car dealership; and Dalbert Chuw, chairman of China-Australia trade. And now it is my great pleasure to introduce you to the best of the best: our top twelve finalists! Take it away, number Two-One-Seven. Marcy Liang.

Note: Actors begin doubling in the following sequence.

MARCY *sashays.*

ZHEN HUA: Number Eleven. Joy Kwan.

JOY *prances around.*

Number Sixty-Nine. Sabrina Choi.

SABRINA *krumps.*

Number Thirty-Six. Pauline Kwok.

PAULINE KWOK *does cutesy hearts.*

Number One-Nine-Two. Heidi Ma.

HEIDI MA *flexes her muscles.*

Number Six. Jessica Wong.

JESSICA WONG *mimes. The buzzer sounds—she's been eliminated. She mimes her way offstage.*

Number One-Oh-Four. Cloudie Qin.

CLOUDIE QIN *throws kisses to the audience.*

Number Seventy-Seven. Rowena Chan.

ROWENA CHAN *prowls like a tiger.*

Number Two-Six-Oh. Flora Teo.

FLORA TEO *enters half-dressed. The buzzer sounds—she's been eliminated. She screams and runs offstage.*

Number Eighty. Loletta Bai.

LOLETTA BAI *drops her wig. The buzzer sounds—she's been eliminated.*

Number Forty-Seven. Kandice Lau.

KANDICE LAU *is late. The buzzer sounds—she's been eliminated.*

And last but certainly not least, number Eighty-Eight. Lily Fung.

LILY *catwalks nervously, holding back tears.*

The doubling ends.

That was our top twelve! They will return shortly for the glamour round!

SCENE 14

A backstage green room where the women prep.

LILY *enters. She grabs a cheongsam and goes to a changeroom.*

LILY: [*to herself*] I can do this.

> *She stops, hearing voices from the changeroom.*

JOY: [*in Mandarin*] 對了。就是那裡。太好了。 (That's it. Right there, that's good.)

MARCY: [*in Mandarin*] 你想要快一点还是慢一点？ (Do you want it faster or slower?)

JOY: [*in Mandarin*] 試著快一點！ (Try going faster!)

LILY: Hello?

> LILY *pulls the changeroom curtain back, revealing* MARCY *and* JOY *making out.*

LILY: OH MY GOD!

JOY: CHANGE ROOM BUSY!

> MARCY *pulls the curtain shut so only their heads are visible.*

LILY: I'M SO SORRY! I SHOULD HAVE KNOCKED!

JOY: Don't worry! You can't knock on curtain. Are you okay, Lily? You look upset. Like you been crying all night with big puff around your eyeballs.

LILY: I'm fine. I'm not crying.

> MARCY *and* JOY *step out of the changeroom.*

MARCY: You're not mad, are you? We wanted to tell you and Sabrina.

LILY: Why would I be mad?

MARCY: I didn't want you to think that just because I'm in love with Joy that we would turn against you and Sabrina in the competition.

JOY: [*in Mandarin*] 你愛我？ (You love me?)

LILY: I'm happy for you both, and I'm sure Sabrina will be too! Sorry, but I really have to get changed—

> LILY *steps into the changeroom.*

JOY: Thank you, Lily! I'm so relief!

MARCY: Me too, but can you keep it a secret for now, Lily?

JOY: [*in Mandarin*] 我們為甚麼要保守秘密？難道你不想在一起嗎？ (Why do we have to be a secret? Don't you want to be together?)

MARCY: [*in Mandarin*] 我当然想啊！你知道的。但是这对我来讲太恐怖了，我需要一点时间。我的家人还不知道呢。 (Of course I do! You know that. But this is scary for me and I need time. My family doesn't know.)

A beat.

JOY: [*in Mandarin*] 我明白的。你只能按照自己的步伐前進。 (I understand. You can only do this at your own pace.)

MARCY: [*in Mandarin*] 我真是个白痴！我早就知道听随自己的心意会令你受伤，看看现在发生了甚么！请你不要放弃寻找真爱。可能你的真命天女今晚正在观看牡丹小姐呢。你值得一个和你同样完美的人。 (I'm a fool! I knew that if I gave into my feelings that you would get hurt and now look what's happened! Please don't give up on your dream of meeting someone. Maybe the right woman for you is watching Miss Peony tonight. You deserve to be with someone amazing who is on your level.)

JOY: [*in Mandarin*] 我還以為自己已經找到一個完美的人了。 (I thought I'd found someone amazing already.)

MARCY: [*in Mandarin*] Joy，我很对不起你。 (I'm so sorry, Joy.)

JOY: [*in Mandarin*] 你不需要為任何事情感到抱歉。 (You don't need to be sorry for anything.)

JOY *kisses* MARCY *on the cheek and leaves.* LILY *joins* MARCY, *half-dressed.*

LILY: Where did Joy go?

MARCY: Do you ever wish you could go back in time? So you could have one more chance to … be in that moment when you see someone for the first time—I mean, really see them. There is a split second where the mist clears, and you realise this person is the centre point of everything that matters. Knowing them fills you with relief and dread. What if they disappear? You hold those states of gratitude and fear in suspense until one day you lose sight, your arms give way—and things break apart.

MARCY leaves. LILY *feels Adeline's presence but cannot see her. She tries piecing the broken pieces of the jade bracelet together.*

LILY: Please come back. I should have listened to you. I should have practised your dance more. Look at me: I can't even do up my dress.

SABRINA rushes past spritzing herself with hairspray.

SABRINA: This is more insane than Defqon! Lily, what's wrong?

LILY: Please help me.

SABRINA helps LILY *into her dress.*

SABRINA: Hey! Stand up straight. Shoulders back. You're looking good. You're Adeline Yu's granddaughter, remember! Here, just let me fix your camel toe.

She sprays Lily's crotch with hairspray.

We've got you.

SCENE 15

A spotlight on ZHEN HUA *as he sings the ballad 'Love Confession' by Jay Chou in Mandarin. As he sings, he dances with each of the contestants.*

MARCY *enters and tries throwing Ausway coupons into the audience.* ZHEN HUA *confiscates them.*

MARCY *exits. She brushes shoulders with* JOY *on the way out, looks back at* JOY *longingly as* JOY *dances with* ZHEN HUA.

JOY *exits.* SABRINA *enters and goes a bit too hard on the dance floor.*

SABRINA *exits.* LILY *enters and she and* ZHEN HUA *share an unexpectedly tender moment while dancing.*

LILY *and* ZHEN HUA *become lost in the moment until the song ends.* ZHEN HUA *snaps himself out of it and speaks to the crowd.*

ZHEN HUA: You're watching this year's Miss Peony Grand Final at Galaxies Casino. When we return, our finalists will be partaking in the charisma and talent rounds! From calligraphy to traditional fan dancing—we have it all. Don't go away.

LILY: Fan dancing?! Oh god!

LILY panics and exits.

SCENE 16

Backstage.

MARCY, JOY *and* SABRINA *tidy themselves as* LILY *tries piecing together the broken pieces of the jade bracelet.*

LILY: Por Por! I haven't practised your fan dance enough!

JOY: Hurry, Lily! Commercial break will end soon!

SABRINA: Lily, you can buy another bracelet!

LILY: I need this bracelet!

MARCY: I'll get you jade from Ausway! Half price!

LILY: This one belonged to my grandmother. I can't do that fan dance without her. I can't do any of this without her!

SABRINA: I know you're still grieving and it must be heaps hard not having her around—

LILY: I have had her around.

MARCY: You've kept her in your heart, yes. That's very special.

LILY: No. She's been with me since the pageant started.

MARCY: What are you talking about?

LILY: This is going to be sound unbelievable, but—my grandmother is haunting me from purgatory. She can't pass into the afterlife until I fulfill a promise I made about Miss Peony. Before, I just wanted to escape somewhere else, anywhere else, but now I don't give a shit about London! None of that matters if I've lost her soul—I'd never be able to forgive myself. This bracelet … it belonged to my Por Por and when I wear it, she appears. But last night, we had the worst fight and she said the most horrible things. I got so angry that I broke it and killed her! She's dead! Again! What if I've sent her to hell?

> MARCY *and* SABRINA *exchange worried looks;* LILY *has clearly lost it.* JOY *sits in a corner by herself, eating a banana.*

JOY: I wondered who was that old woman.

LILY: You could see her too!

JOY: I see lots of people. Chit-chat. Make friends. There are three ghosts here right now. [*To no-one*] Hello Jennifer. Hello Haruka. Achu, you looking very nice.

MARCY: So, Adeline Yu has been helping you?

SABRINA: YOU MEAN TO TELL ME—

LILY: I know you must all feel cheated—

SABRINA: YOU'RE SAYING THAT ADELINE YU HAS SEEN ME ONSTAGE? THE ADELINE YU? OH MY GOD I NEED MORE DEODORANT, I CANNOT BELIEVE THIS!!!

JOY: [*to Lily*] What was your promise about Miss Peony?

LILY: I promised that I would win the pageant.

The women fall silent. A long beat. Eventually, JOY *claps her hands resolutely and starts rummaging through drawers.*

What are you doing?

JOY: [*in Mandarin*] 我之前見過一個打火機。我們要召喚她婆婆。 (I saw a lighter in here before. We need to summon her grandmother.)

MARCY: [*in Mandarin*] 然后让她和Lily赢下比赛？你在说笑吧！ (So she and Lily can win? You can't be serious!)

JOY: [*in Mandarin*] 她們需要我們的幫助！現在要對付的是靈界和常人未能理解的生物。這可能是我們有生以來最有意義的經歷。或者，這就是我們都被吸引來參選牡丹小姐的原由吧。這是命運，是緣分。 (They need our help! We're dealing with the spirit world and matters beyond human comprehension. This could be the most meaningful experience of our lives. Perhaps it's even the reason we were drawn to Miss Peony to begin with. Call it fate. Yuanfen.)

MARCY: [*in Mandarin*] 如果你错了怎么办？我们其他人跟Lily一样非常需要那个皇冠！ (But what if you're wrong?! The rest of us need that crown as much as Lily does!)

SABRINA: Joy, I get that hauntings are heaps serious and I don't want to be cursed for life or anything but if we bring Adeline Yu back Lily's gonna sweep the floor with us. It's not fair.

LILY: Are you performing a séance?!

JOY: [*in Mandarin*] Sabrina你還能夠贏的！我們都是具備競爭力的對手。這不是在給Lily故意放水，而是在拯救她婆婆的魂魄。你的内心是怎麼想的？ (You can still win, Sabrina! We're all fierce competitors. This isn't about trying to give Lily an advantage; it's about saving her grandmother's soul. What does your heart tell you?)

After a long beat, MARCY *and* SABRINA *start helping* JOY *in her search.*

MARCY: [*in Mandarin*] 我们还需要甚么？ (What else do we need?)

SABRINA: I found the lighter! And some paper!

JOY: [*in Mandarin*] 快把垃圾桶拿過來，放在那邊！ (Get that rubbish can and put it over there!)

LILY: What is going on?!

JOY: We going to summon your Por Por.

LILY: Why are you helping me? Marcy?

MARCY: You're our friend, Lily. I already lost Joy. I don't want to lose you too.

LILY: Sabrina?

SABRINA: [*not listening*] I'M GONNA MEET ADELINE YU. SOMEBODY SMELL MY BREATH!

JOY: Lily, give me bracelet.

> JOY *lights the paper and lays the bracelet pieces in the ashes. She instructs the other women how to bow. For a beat, nothing happens. And then suddenly* ADELINE *appears. They all scream.*

LILY: Por Por!

JOY: Aunty.

MARCY: Aunty.

SABRINA: AUNTY MY NAME IS SABRINA AND I'M A HUGE FAN.

ADELINE: [*in Cantonese*] 你哋成班女仔喺度食煙呀？ (Are you girls smoking?)

LILY: No, it's joss paper! Kind of. I broke your bracelet but my friends helped me summon you from the spirit world!

ADELINE: [*in Cantonese*] 你冇召喚我。 (You didn't summon me.)

LILY: But the bracelet—?

ADELINE: [*in Cantonese*] 手握嚟㗎咋嘛？點控制到我呢！我返嚟係因為我有說話想同你講。 (It's just a bracelet! It can't control me! I came back because I needed to talk to you.)

LILY: So you were just giving me the silent treatment? That's such a typical elder move!

ADELINE: [*in Cantonese*] 唔係！我只係需要啲時間諗清楚啫。對你講啲咁難聽嘅說話係我嘅錯。要令到我承認呢樣嘢其實好難，真係活到老學到老啊，死咗做隻鬼都仲學緊嘢。你同你嘅朋友願意企出嚟反抗林百祥係一件好事。你有勇氣去做一啲我都做唔到嘅嘢。唔到我唔認一你真係似足我呀。你阿媽

以前成日話我哋鬧交係因為大家都死牛一面頸。我知，無論幾大犧牲，你都嘗試過冚我。我仲記得你嗰陣唔再講廣東話而去專心學英文係為咗唔俾班澳洲鬼仔蝦你。當時我唔明你左右為難，俾兩邊扯到哗唔到氣，爭啲連你自己都消失埋。係你最需要我支持嘅時候，我並冇喺你身邊幫你。相反，我推得你越嚟越遠。但係其實你一直都已經做得夠好。我相信你只要做自己就可以贏㗎喇。 (No! I needed some time to think. I was wrong to say those harsh things. It's difficult for me to admit this but even as a spirit I'm still learning. It's good you and your friends stood up against Ken Lam. You had the courage to do what I couldn't. And you are like me—painfully so. Your mother used to say we clashed because we're both so stubborn. I know you've tried hard to please me, even when it cost you dearly. I remember when you stopped speaking Cantonese to focus on learning English so the Australian kids would stop teasing you. I didn't understand then that you were being pulled in two different directions, pulled so thin you almost disappeared. When you were struggling, you needed my support. Instead, I ended up pushing you away. But you were always enough. I believe you can win just as you are.)

LILY *wipes her eyes.* ADELINE *shooshes her.*

[*In Cantonese*] 傻豬嚟嘅，唔好喊。快啲去完成你開始咗嘅嘢喇。 (Silly pig. Don't cry. Go and finish what you started.)

SCENE 17

On stage, ZHEN HUA *holds a stack of palm cards.*

ZHEN HUA: Welcome back to the Grand Final of Miss Peony! If you're just joining us—lucky you, we're only halfway through the charisma round. Here, the charm and quick-wittedness of the contestants is tested when they must spruik a product to the judges! The catch? They don't know what that product is yet! Next up: contestant number Sixty-Nine.

SABRINA *enters.* ZHEN HUA *reads from a palm card.*

Your object is a blank notebook. Your time starts now!

SABRINA: [*in Cantonese*] 有咗呢一本咁實用嘅白間薄，你可以用你最鍾意嘅原子筆或者鉛筆記錄低你最瘋狂嘅夢想。我相信

只要你向宇宙許願，宇宙就會回應你㗎喇。上年我開始寫日記，每一晚我都會寫低我想贏得牡丹小姐冠軍嘅夢想。依家睇下我，入圍咗總決賽！咁你試諗下，一本全新嘅筆記簿可以實現到你幾多想要嘅嘢。 (With a practical, blank notebook you can put your favourite pen or pencil to the page and record your wildest dreams. I'm a firm believer that if you put a request out into the universe, the universe will provide. Last year, I kept a diary, and each night I would write about my dream of winning Miss Peony. And here I am! A Grand Finalist! Just think of what you could achieve with a new notebook.)

SABRINA *does a 'West Side' symbol and exits.* MARCY *enters.*

ZHEN HUA: Wonderful, number Sixty-Nine! Now, contestant Two-One-Seven. Your object is a pair of men's dress shoes. Your time starts now.

MARCY: [*in Mandarin*] 谁会不想在一天漫长劳碌的工作后，回家脱掉一对美丽的皮鞋，然后享受着妻子的脚底按摩呢？每个男人都有权力享有国王级的待遇，只要你拥有了这一对皮鞋，你永远都不会被误认为乡村野民。无论是在办公室内、高尔夫球场上或者是在绅士俱乐部里拿着最喜欢的威士忌，你都将踏着时尚的步伐，舒适地迈步向前。 (Who wouldn't want a beautiful pair of shoes to kick off at the end of the day so his wife can give him a foot rub after a long shift at work? Every man deserves to be treated like a king and with a pair of dress shoes you'll never be mistaken for peasantry. Walk in style and comfort, whether it's at the office, on the golf course, or at the gentleman's club with your favourite whisky!)

MARCY *bows and exits.* JOY *enters.*

ZHEN HUA: Thank you, number Two-One-Seven. Is there a Mister Two-One-Seven? Please welcome contestant number Eleven! Your object is a brown onion.

JOY: [*in Mandarin*] 洋蔥？是的。我最喜歡的食物是蔬菜。不管是甚麼種類：蘿蔔、西葫蘆、蔥、菜薊—所有我都愛吃。但是不知為何，我一直對洋蔥有強烈的厭惡。我覺得洋蔥防禦性高、又冷漠。每次碰面都總是會發生爭辯。但隨著時光飛逝，我驚訝地發現我慢慢喜歡上洋蔥。只要適當地烹煮和醃製，洋蔥可以令每道佳餚更鮮甜。配合適當的儲存方法，洋蔥既耐存又貼心，更是美味。逐漸，洋蔥便成為了我最喜歡

的蔬菜。我每天都想吃洋蔥。現在不管如何,我最愛洋蔥了。 (An onion? Yes. My favourite food is vegetables. It doesn't matter what kind: carrot, zucchini, leek, artichoke—I love them all. But for some reason, I have always had a strong dislike for onion. I found onion to be defensive and cold and debated with onion each time we met. But over time, and to my surprise, I grew to like onion. When cooked and marinated properly, onion made every dish sweeter. When stored correctly, onion was hardy and caring, and delicious. Eventually, onions became my favourite vegetable. I wanted onion every day. Now, despite everything, I love onion.)

JOY *exits and* LILY *enters.*

ZHEN HUA: Will somebody get this woman a bag of onions! She's onion-obsessed! Thank you, number Eleven. And finally, contestant number Eighty-Eight. Your object is a naked flame.

As LILY *speaks, she begins taking apart her* ADELINE *look— rubbing off her lipstick and revealing her tattoos.*

LILY: The thing about fire is that it has the potential to be life-giving as well as destructive. Kind of like Miss Peony. The life-giving parts of this pageant have been the women I've met, the friends I've made. But the destructive parts … the gatekeeping, the rejection. What gives you the right to decide if someone qualifies as Chinese? What's with the exclusivity? I feel as out of place in this community as my grandmother did when she arrived in Australia.

Play-off music begins playing.

We spend so much time as Chinese people thinking it's us versus Westerners that we forget that sometimes it's us versus us—the factions of Chineseness that are separated by culture, nationality, and race, facing off against each other.

The play-off music gets louder.

It's like, 'Here are the ABCs' and 'Here are the new arrivals', and never the two shall meet. Do you know why the majority love infighting within minority groups? Because it distracts us from dismantling the system they created to repress us all.

LILY*'s mic gets cut.*

Miss Peony has the potential to be something truly welcoming. In its ideal form, any of us could win. In its ideal form, I could be Miss Peony.

LILY *exits.*

SCENE 18

Backstage.

LILY *paces. The other women rush in.*

LILY: That was stupid of me. That was really stupid.

MARCY: Lily, it was amazing.

JOY: So wonderful, Lily. I agree that we need more acceptance of each other. More focus on celebrate our difference.

SABRINA: I totally know what you mean about the exclusion, too. I feel it every time I go to a Chinese restaurant and they give me a fork to eat with after they hear my Aussie accent. A fork!

JOY: You should be proud of yourself, Lily.

LILY: Thanks. But I don't think I stand a chance of winning after that. And then what will happen to my Por Por?

ZHEN HUA *enters. The women surround him.*

ZHEN HUA: They've cancelled the talent round. They've gone into damage control and want to speed up the ceremony, so the winner will be announced after the commercial break.

MARCY: Has Lily been eliminated?

ZHEN HUA *nods. The women fire up.*

JOY: Is your fault! All the judges think like you!

ZHEN HUA: Joy, I'm sorry. About everything. And I didn't want Lily to be eliminated either but it wasn't my choice.

ADELINE *appears.*

ADELINE: [*in Cantonese*] 其實，你有得揀㗎。 (You do have a choice, actually.)

ZHEN HUA *screams.*

ZHEN HUA: WHAT—WHAT IS HAPPENING?

MARCY: It's just a ghost Zhen Hua, get over yourself!

ZHEN HUA: WHO ARE YOU?

SABRINA: She's Lily's Por Por who's been haunting her since she died because of an unfulfilled promise—she won't be able to pass peacefully into the afterlife until Lily wins Miss Peony except now Lily's screwed up 'cause she was honest about her life experience, oh my god catch up Zhen Hua.

ADELINE: [*in Cantonese*] 振華，你要對評判嘅決定提出質疑。 (Zhen Hua, you are going to contest the judge's decision.)

ZHEN HUA: Me? I don't have any power!

JOY: You the producer! Tell them Lily stay otherwise we all quit!

MARCY: Uh, what?

SABRINA: Yeah, what?

ADELINE: [*in Cantonese*] 佢哋全部都退賽嘅話仲大件事呀。如果今年澳洲牡丹小姐冇冠軍去北京做代表參賽，咁成個組織都會好瘀㗎。 (It would be scandalous if they all quit. With no winner of Miss Peony Australia competing in Beijing this year, the organisation would lose face.)

LILY: And it would be your fault.

ZHEN HUA: The judges won't listen to me!

ADELINE: [*in Cantonese*] 你要試下。 (You need to try.)

JOY: You owe us.

ZHEN HUA: What if it doesn't work—what do I say to them—this isn't protocol—

LILY: CAN YOU JUST—

> LILY *kisses* ZHEN HUA, *giving him a boost of courage.*

THERE. TRY.

ZHEN HUA: I'll, I'll try to convince them!

> ZHEN HUA *makes a phone call. The conversation can't be heard, but we can see what he's dealing with—frustration, anger, bargaining. The women watch him, on tenterhooks, until he finally hangs up.*

ZHEN HUA: I'm so sorry, Lily …

LILY: No.

SABRINA: Are you serious!

JOY: Try again!

MARCY: Call them back!

ZHEN HUA: I'm so sorry … because you've only got a minute left to tidy up for the announcement since you're still in the running!

LILY *faux attacks* ZHEN HUA *who doesn't fight back, enjoying the attention from her. The other women celebrate.*

LILY: [*to Zhen Hua*] OH MY GOD! DON'T EVER DO THAT AGAIN.

SCENE 19

On stage, the women hold hands. ZHEN HUA *reads from a card. Drum rolls.*

ZHEN HUA: And now for the moment we've all been waiting for: the announcement of the runners-up and the winner of this year's Miss Peony! Our third runner-up, whose prize consists of a year's supply of TumTum toilet tissue is … contestant number Eleven! Congratulations Joy Kwan!

Spotlight on JOY. *The women applaud.*

Our second runner-up, who wins ten teeth-whitening sessions at Harmony Dental Chatswood is … contestant number Two-One-Seven! Congratulations Marcy Liang!

Spotlight on MARCY. *The women applaud.*

And our first runner-up, who receives a five-thousand-dollar voucher for Longli Supermarkets, and who will undertake the responsibilities of the winner if, under any circumstance, the winner is unable to fulfill her duties … contestant number Eighty-Eight. Lily Fung.

Spotlight on LILY. *She applauds* SABRINA, *genuinely happy for her.* MARCY, JOY *and* ZHEN HUA *are conflicted but follow* LILY's *lead.*

Which means, the winner of this year's pageant, and your new Miss Peony, who will go on to compete for the international crown in Beijing later this year is Sabrina Choi. Contestant number Sixty-Nine.

SABRINA *is crowned and handed an enormous bouquet of peonies. She sobs.*

SABRINA: Sixty-Nine! NICE!

SCENE 20

Late that evening in the casino conference hall. The set and decorations have been cleared away from the stage. LILY *finds* ADELINE *alone, quietly performing her fan dance before a crackling firepit. When she sees* LILY, *she stops dancing.*

LILY: Por Por?

ADELINE: [*in Cantonese*] 你做得好好呀，冬冬。 (You competed well, Dong Dong.)

> *They stand side by side, at a loss.*

LILY: What's going to happen to you?

ADELINE: [*in Cantonese*] 我都唔係好知呀。我估你以後去邊我 都要跟住你㗎喇。 (I'm not entirely sure. I guess I must follow wherever you go.)

LILY: That won't be such a bad thing.

ADELINE: [*in Cantonese*] 唯一嘅問題係當你同你阿媽全部都去曬， 我哋就無得喺下面一家團聚。到時我唔哚唔吊咁，實好難挨 呀。我會好掛住你哋㗎。 (The only problem is that once you all die—you, your mother—we won't get to be together. I'll still be in limbo. That will be hard. I will miss you very much.)

> LILY *tears up and* ADELINE *gently shooshes her. After a beat,* LILY *performs part of Adeline's fan dance. It's more beautiful than either of them expect.*

[*In Cantonese*] 係啦。嗱啦 …但係你仲要練習下伸展嘅動作。 (Ah. There it is … But you need to work on your extension.)

> *They laugh.*

[*In Cantonese*] 喺呢啲時候，令到我諗番起李白首詩。你明唔 明佢咩意思呀？ (At times like these, I'm reminded of Li Bai's poem. Do you know what it means?)

LILY: [*in Cantonese*] 床前明月光，疑是地上霜。舉頭望明月，低 頭思故鄉。 ('At the foot of my bed there is moonlight / It looks like frost on the ground / I raise my head to look at the moon / I lower my head and think of home.') He's lonely. He wishes he hadn't been separated from his family and his home. Did you ever miss Hong Kong when you were alive?

ADELINE: [*in Cantonese*] 有你呢隻傻豬喺度點會咧。 (Not when I had my silly pig.)

LILY *starts.*

LILY: Por Por! You're disappearing!

ADELINE: [*in Cantonese*] 係咩？係喎！阿彌陀佛。我終於會見番阿爸阿媽、兄弟姊妹，可以同埋班老友記打下麻雀啦！冬冬—記得清明嗰陣喺倫敦要拜下我呀！仲有記住歐洲同澳洲有時差㗎，唔好搞錯！唉仲有！記得你要帶齊啲啱嘅供品，咁到時我落到去都住得舒服啲—衣食住行搞掂咗咪可以保佑你哋全家平平安安行大運！你阿媽知我最鍾意飲邊隻白蘭地！到時你移咗民，就算要飛幾耐都好，要多啲返嚟探下佢。光陰似箭呀，同大家相處嘅時間好寶貴㗎。 (I am? I AM! OH THANK GOD. I'm going to see my parents. My siblings. Play mah jong with old school friends! Dong Dong—make sure you pray to me from London during Ching Ming! And make sure you get the date right because of the time difference between Europe and Australia! And oh! Make sure you bring the right offerings so I can live the high life in the spirit world—eating and drinking and bringing luck and prosperity to you all! Your mother knows my favourite type of brandy! Once you move, you need to visit her regularly, even with the long-haul flight. Life is fleeting, and our time with each other is precious.)

LILY: How is this happening? I didn't win Miss Peony!

ADELINE: [*in Cantonese*] 我哋梗係理解錯咗嗰個承諾啦。 (We must have misunderstood the promise.)

LILY: I promised I would win.

ADELINE: [*in Cantonese*] 你應承咗會繼承我嘅遺志 … 從來都唔係話要贏得啲咩比賽或者做一個最「叻」嘅華人。當我嚟到呢個國家嘅時候，我成立咗牡丹小姐呢個比賽去保護我自己同埋社區入面我關懷嘅人，令到佢哋可以唔洗驚做最真實嘅自己。牡丹小姐嘅創立都係為咗慶祝今日既我。 (You promised to honour my legacy … which has never been about winning competitions or being the 'best' Chinese person. When I came to this country, I started Miss Peony to protect myself and the people

I loved so they could be the truest versions of themselves without fear. I started Miss Peony as a celebration of who I am.)

> ADELINE *is almost completely gone now.*

LILY: I was just getting to know you.

ADELINE: [*in Cantonese*] 我哋已經成為咗彼此嘅一部分。傻豬。 (We are part of each other. Silly pig.)

> ADELINE *holds her hand out.* LILY *tries to take it, but they cannot touch.* ADELINE *disappears. Suddenly,* LILY *feels something in her pocket—it's the jade bracelet, magically mended. She puts it on but* ADELINE *doesn't appear. She sits.* ZHEN HUA *joins her.*

LILY: How are they all going?

ZHEN HUA: Sabrina's wasted and Joy and Marcy are hooking up in my car.

LILY: Oh my god.

> *They laugh.*

ZHEN HUA: Is your Por Por here?

LILY: Not anymore.

ZHEN HUA: Are you okay?

LILY: [*nodding*] Will the pageant be okay?

ZHEN HUA: Well Ken Lam's withdrawn his funding, but Marcy's family stepped in and offered to be primary sponsors. Apparently Ausway sales are through the roof thanks to her non-stop promoting.

LILY: There you go! Many more years of Miss Peony to come, then.

ZHEN HUA: Yep. But not with me running it; I'm not renewing my contract. After everything that happened with Ken Lam—I think I lost my way. What was it you said to me? 'Men like you shouldn't run Miss Peony.'

LILY: I was only echoing what you said to me. That girls like me don't win Miss Peony.

ZHEN HUA: I should never have said that. I really admired your honesty in the charisma round. It was brave and kind of distilled the toxic aspects of the community. And um, about that kiss. Don't worry, I didn't think anything of it. I know it must have been in the heat of the moment when you wanted my help so—

> LILY *kisses* ZHEN HUA. *When they pull apart,* ZHEN HUA *stands and rearranges his pants—he's got a semi-erection.*

I'm just gonna, I'll go get us some drinks. You want a drink? I need one.

> ZHEN HUA *exits, hobbling.* MARCY *and* JOY *enter, holding hands.* SABRINA *follows soon after, wearing her crown.*

LILY: Hey, Miss Peonies.

> *They huddle close to* LILY *and then look around, searching for* ADELINE.

JOY: Your Por Por gone?

SABRINA: I didn't get an autograph!!

MARCY: How did you do it?

LILY: It was never about winning the pageant. It was about … being authentic.

> JOY *hugs* LILY.

JOY: We so happy for you, Lily. But now that Miss Peony finish, you going to leave us. When you flying to London town?

LILY: I cancelled my flights. I'll lose the deposit on my flat and I'll have to get my things shipped home, but that's okay.

SABRINA: What are you going to do now?

LILY: Well, managing the bar has been fun but there's not much meaning in it for me anymore. Apparently, they're looking for a new producer for Miss Peony so I think I'll apply for that. There's so much to love about the pageant but there's a lot of room for improvement. Maybe with someone like me producing, the pageant could become a better version of itself. Maybe what it means to be Miss Peony could expand. But I'll need some guidance from some trusted friends along the way …

> *The women chitter excitedly.*

JOY: So you staying in Australia with us!

MARCY: Excellent choice! [*in Mandarin*] 英国本来就很糟糕。你还记得当时鸦片战争他们是怎么对待我们的吗？ (England is terrible anyway. Do you remember what they did to us during the Opium war?)

SABRINA: OH MY GOD LILY YOU'LL TOTALLY GET THE JOB AND THEN YOU'LL BE ON THE CIRCUIT WITH ME! I'M SO STOKED! LET'S DO SHOTS!!!

The other women exit, led by SABRINA. LILY *hangs back to watch the firepit, uses it to light a cigarette. As it burns,* ADELINE*'s voice echoes in the air.*

ADELINE: [*in Cantonese*] 冬冬 … (Dong Dong …)

LILY: Okay. No smoking. Couldn't go quietly, could you?

LILY *stubs the cigarette and watches the fire, smiling.*

THE END

Thank you to Belvoir St Theatre's supporters – our donors, giving circles, trusts & foundations and partners – for helping us to create brilliant works of theatre.

Miss Peony was presented on the Belvoir St Theatre mainstage in the 2023 Season with thanks to the support of the Nelson Meers Foundation and Creative Development Fund, and in association with Arts Centre Melbourne, Asia TOPA and Queensland Performing Arts Centre. *Miss Peony* was developed in partnership with Playwriting Australia.

NELSON MEERS FOUNDATION

Arts Centre Melbourne

ASIATOPA

qpac QUEENSLAND PERFORMING ARTS CENTRE

playwriting australia

BELVOIR ST THEATRE

Based in an old factory on Gadigal land, Sydney, Belvoir is one of Australia's most celebrated and beloved theatre companies. Since 1984, when a group of 600 theatre-lovers came together to buy a theatre and save it from becoming an apartment block, Belvoir has been at the forefront of Australian storytelling for the stage. Each year the company presents an annual season of shows for this now-iconic corner stage. New work and new stories sit at the centre of Belvoir's programming, alongside a mix of reinvented classics and international writing, and a foundational commitment to Indigenous stories. In short, Belvoir is about theatrical invention, an open society, and faith in humanity.

Under the leadership of Artistic Director Eamon Flack and Executive Director Aaron Beach, Belvoir engages Australia's most prominent and promising theatre-makers.

Belvoir has nurtured the talents of artists including Cate Blanchett, Simon Stone, Leah Purcell, Benedict Andrews, Tommy Murphy, Kate Mulvany, Anne-Louise Sarks, Wesley Enoch, S. Shakthidharan, and former Artistic Director Neil Armfield. Landmark productions include Counting and Cracking, *The Wild Duck, FANGIRLS, Cloudstreet, Barbara and the Camp Dogs, The Drover's Wife, The Glass Menagerie, Angels in America, Keating!, The Sapphires*, and many, many more. Belvoir regularly tours nationally and internationally.

Belvoir receives government support for its activities from the Federal Government through the Australia Council and the state government through Create NSW.

belvoir.com.au

BELVOIR SUPPORTERS

We are deeply grateful to our community for their unwavering support enabling us to continue to the Belvoir tradition of creating brilliant, playful and thought-provoking works of theatre. Your faith in us has made all the difference. Thank you.

PATRONS

Her Excellency the Honourable Margaret Beazley AC KC Governor of New South Wales.

BELVOIR BOARD (CO.B)

Patricia Akopiantz *Deputy Chair*
Raji Ambikairajah
Johanna Featherstone
Alison Kitchen
Michael Lynch CBE AO
Sam Meers AO *Chair*
Jacob Nash
Paul Oppenheim
Mark Warburton

BELVOIR BOARD (CO.A)

Amitav Goswami
Ian Learmonth
Stuart Mccreery
Angela Pearman *Chair*
Sue Rosen
Nick Schlieper
Mark Seymour
Susan Teasey

TRUSTS AND FOUNDATIONS

Andrew Cameron Family Foundation
Blake Beckett Trust
Copyright Agency Cultural Fund
Doc Ross Family Foundation
Gandevia Foundation

The Greatorex Fund
The Macquarie Group Foundation
The Neilson Foundation
Oranges & Sardines
The Wales Family Foundation

BELVOIR GIVING CIRCLES

CHAIR'S CIRCLE

Led by Sam Meers, the Chair's Circle supports an iconic Belvoir show each year, including *The Cherry Orchard* (2021), *The Jungle and the Sea* (2022) and *Into the Woods* (2023).

Patty Akopiantz & Justin Punch
Robert & Libby Albert
Sophie & Stephen Allen
Diane Balnaves
Hamish Balnaves
Guido Belgiorno-Nettis AM & Michelle Belgiorno-Nettis
Anne Britton
Jillian Broadbent AC FRSN
Andrew Cameron AM & Cathy Cameron
David Gonski AC & Associate Professor Orli Wargon OAM
Fee & David Hancock
Alison Kitchen
Ian Learmonth & Julia Pincus
Helen Lynch AM & Helen Bauer
Tom Mcfarlane
Carole Meers
Sam Meers AO
Kerr Neilson
Stuart & Kate O'Brien
Paul & Cathie Oppenheim
Daniel & Jackie Phillips
Andrew Price
Sherry-Hogan Foundation
Rob Thomas AO
The WeirAnderson Foundation
Wiggs Foundation
Kim Williams AM & Catherine Dovey
Rosie Williams & John Grill
Cathy Yuncken

THE GROUP

The Group is a collective of inspiring likeminded women committed to supporting female creatives and bringing more women's stories to the Belvoir stage, including *Stop Girl* (2021), *Tell Me I'm Here* (2022), and *The Weekend* (2023).

Patty Akopiantz
Sophie Allen
Katrina Barter
Jessica Block
Catherine Brenner
Sally Cousens
Kirsty Gold
Robin Low
Sam Meers AO
Sarah Meers
Naomi O'Brien
Rebel Penfold-Russell OAM
Alisa Pincus
Louise Thurgood-Phillips

BELVOIR DONORS

Thank you to the visionary donors who have committed to a level of financial support that allows us to realise our creative ambitions and share passionate, diverse and surprising contemporary Australian theatre with audiences here, across the country and across the globe.

$50,000 AND ABOVE

Andrew Cameron AM & Cathy Cameron
David Gonski AC & Associate Professor Orli Wargon OAM
Sam Meers AO
Professor Cav. Simon Mordant AO & Catriona Mordant AM
The Balnaves Foundation
Nelson Meers Foundation
The Neilson Foundation
Ord Minnett
Ian Potter Foundation

$20,000-$49,999

Patty Akopiantz & Justin Punch
Aldus Group
Blake Beckett Trust
Copyright Agency Cultural Fund
David and Fee Hancock Foundation
Doc Ross Family Foundation
Marion Heathcote & Brian Burfitt
Houston Group
Ingrid Kaiser
Lazberger Family Fund
Ian Learmonth & Julia Pincus
Neilson Foundation
Oranges & Sardines

$10,000-$19,999

Robert & Libby Albert
Sophie & Stephen Allen
Guido Belgiorno-Nettis AM & Michelle Belgiorno-Nettis
Ellen Borda
Anne Britton
Jillian Broadbent AC FRSN
Bob & Chris Ernst
Gandevia Foundation
Libby Higgin & Dr Gae Anderson
Kimberley and Angus Holden
Alison Kitchen
Ross Littlewood & Alexandra Curtain
Helen Lynch AM & Helen Bauer
M&C Saatchi
Robert and Vanessa Morgan
Paul and Cathie Oppenheim
Rebel Penfold-Russell OAM
Daniel and Jackie Phillips
Rachel Emma Ferguson Foundation
The Roberts Pike Foundation
Rob Thomas AO
The Wales Family Foundation
The WeirAnderson Foundation
Sally White
Rosie Williams and John Grill AO

SPECIAL THANKS

We also thank our Life Members, who have made outstanding contributions to Belvoir over more than thirty years. They have changed the course of the company and are now ingrained in its fabric.

Neil Armfield AO, Neil Balnaves AO, Andrew Cameron AM, David Gonski AC, Rachel Healy, Louise Herron AM, Sue Hill, Geoffrey Rush AC, Orli Wargon OAM and Chris Westwood.

We would also like to acknowledge Len Armfield, Brian Carey, Sharan Daly, Nick Enright, Ronald Falk, Diane Hague, Jann Kohlman, Cajetan Mula, Geoffrey Scharer and Ronald Thompson, who made a dramatic difference by remembering Belvoir in their Wills. We will always remember their generosity.

These people and Foundations supported the redevelopment of Belvoir Street Theatre and the purchase of our Warehouse in 2005 & 2006.

Andrew & Cathy Cameron
(Refurbishment of theatre
and warehouse)

Russell Crowe
(Redevelopment of theatre)

The Gonski Foundation
& The Nelson Meers Foundation
(Gonski Meers Foyer)

Andrew & Wendy Hamlin
(Executive Director's office)

Hal Herron
(The Hal Bar)

Geoffrey Rush
(Redevelopment of theatre)

Fred Street AM
(Upstairs dressing room)

BELVOIR PARTNERS

Government Partners

Australian Government | Australia Council for the Arts

NSW GOVERNMENT

Major Partners

Baker McKenzie

EY Building a better working world

WOOLCOTT RESEARCH & ENGAGEMENT

ORD MINNETT

Media Partners

adflow

alphabet.

anthem.

SPECIAL T

Associate Partners

barton deakin Government Relations

KAY & HUGHES

Houston

Youth & Education Partners

AFTT ACADEMY OF FILM THEATRE & TELEVISION

Production Partners

AUDIO VISUAL EVENTS

NCC

REGENTS COURT · EST. 1929 ·

HUNTER VALLEY HOLIDAY HOMES LUXURY & STYLE

Accommodation Partners

HOTEL HACIENDA

Event Partners

bourke street bakery

BECKETT'S BAR + DINING

Coopers

DON GIOVANNI Pizza e Pasta

HANDPICKED

zahli

MERCHANT @GREEN

THE NORFOLK HOUSE · HOTEL · REDFERN · 1927

POOR TOMS

TACOS MUCHACHOS

Wellness Partners

SPS Sydney Physio Solutions

leif

Information accurate as at December 2022

www.currency.com.au

Visit Currency Press' website now to:

- Buy your books online
- Browse through our full list of titles, from plays to screenplays, books on theatre, film and music, and more
- Choose a play for your school or amateur performance group by cast size and gender
- Obtain information about performance rights
- Find out about theatre productions and other performing arts news across Australia
- For students, read our study guides
- For teachers, access syllabus and other relevant information
- Sign up for our email newsletter

The performing arts publisher

www.ingramcontent.com/pod-product-compliance
Lightning Source LLC
Chambersburg PA
CBHW050022090426
42734CB00021B/3381